The Secret of God's Organic Salvation

"The Spirit Himself with Our Spirit"

Witness Lee

Living Stream Ministry
Anaheim, CA • www.lsm.org

© 1996 Living Stream Ministry

First Edition, July 1996.

ISBN 978-1-57593-315-3

Published by

Living Stream Ministry
2431 W. La Palma Ave., Anaheim, CA 92801 U.S.A.
P. O. Box 2121, Anaheim, CA 92814 U.S.A.

Printed in the United States of America

10   11   12   13   14   15   /   12   11   10   9   8   7   6   5

CONTENTS

PREFACE

This book is composed of messages given by Brother Witness Lee in Anaheim, California on May 24-27, 1996.

CHAPTER ONE

THE SECRET OF REGENERATION

OUTLINE

I. The Divine Trinity's seeking of the lost sinners:
   A. The Second of the Divine Trinity, the Son, came to seek the lost sinners outside of them objectively on the cross, as a shepherd seeks his lost sheep—Luke 15:4.
   B. Then the Third of the Divine Trinity, the Spirit, comes to seek the lost sinners with the enlightening Word within them subjectively in their heart, as a woman seeking her lost coin by lighting a lamp—Luke 15:8.
   C. This is the initial sanctification of the Spirit to separate a lost sinner from among all the others unto repentance to God for the receiving of Christ's redemption—1 Pet. 1:2; see Chapter Two, point II.A.1.

II. The secret of regeneration—the first section of God's organic salvation:
   A. The Spirit of reality, who has sanctified the lost sinners unto repentance, comes to convict the sinners:
      1. Concerning sin, which is from Adam.
      2. Concerning righteousness, which is of Christ.
      3. Concerning judgment, which belongs to Satan—John 16:8-11.
   B. That they may be born anew of:
      1. Water (the water of baptism signifying death).
      2. The Spirit (who has sanctified the sinner from

among others, and who is the reality of resurrection) in their spirit enlivened by Christ in resurrection—John 3:3, 5.

C. Through the resurrection of Christ that He may impart the divine life into them as the authority for them to be the children of God, begotten of God as His species—1 Pet. 1:3; John 1:12-13.

Definition:

When Christ was resurrected, all His believers, chosen and given to Him by God, were included in Him. Hence, they were all resurrected with Him (Eph. 2:6) and regenerated through Him that they may have the eternal life as the authority for them to be the children of God as His species.

D. This is "that which is born of the Spirit [the Spirit of God] is spirit [the spirit of a sinner born anew]"—John 3:6b.

E. Such a regeneration, a new birth, is a great washing:

1. Purging the regenerated believer from the oldness of his old creation—Titus 3:5.

2. Reconditioning, remaking, remodeling, our old being in life—Titus 3:5; cf. Matt. 19:28.

Definition:

The Greek word for *regeneration* in Titus 3:5 is different from that for *regenerated* in 1 Peter 1:23. The only other place this word is used is in Matthew 19:28, where it is used for the restoration in the millennium. Here it refers to a change from one state to another. Being born again is the commencing of this change. The washing of regeneration begins with our being born again and continues with the renewing of the Holy Spirit as the process of God's new creation, a process that makes us a new man. It is a kind of reconditioning, remaking, or remodeling, with life.

F. This is to drink the life-giving Spirit (1 Cor. 12:13) as the living water:

1. Which the Lord Jesus gives to a believer regenerated by Him—John 4:10; 7:37.
2. Which is the Spirit flowing as the river of water of life from the throne of God—Rev. 22:1, 17; 21:6.
3. Which will become a spring of water gushing up into eternal life—John 4:14.

G. The experiences of the above points A through F are all by exercising the spirit of a repentant and saved sinner through prayer (Eph. 6:18) to call on the name of the Lord (Rom. 10:13).

H. The experiences of the above points A through F are also by receiving the living and abiding word of God (the word of the Spirit of life—John 6:63)—1 Pet. 1:23.

I. Such a saved one receives the Spirit of sonship in his spirit—Gal. 4:5-6; Rom. 8:15.

J. The Spirit of God with our spirit witnesses that we, the regenerated believers, are the children of God—Rom. 8:16.

K. As many as are led by the Spirit of God, these are the sons of God—Rom. 8:14.

L. Such a regenerated believer in Christ is a part of the bride as the increase of Christ the Bridegroom—John 3:3, 5-6, 29-30.

M. Such a child of God should learn to worship God, who is Spirit, with his regenerated spirit mingled with God's Spirit as one spirit—John 4:24; 1 Cor. 6:17.

N. He should also serve God with his spirit in the gospel—Rom. 1:9; 12:11.

Prayer: Father, we extol You as the Lord of heaven and earth. It is of Your sovereignty that we can have this blending conference. Your blending is our blessing. Your blending is our growing. Your blending is our increasing. Your blending is our building. Your blending is everything to us. We long to be blended in the Body and to be blended as the chosen people, the heavenly citizens. Father, give us the new utterance, the up-to-date utterance, to utter what You have shown us. We are so weak, but we thank You that the indwelling Spirit joins us in our weakness. We trust in You and we rely upon You. We ask You to defeat Your enemy and to cover us against all his attacks. Amen.

The burden of these messages can be expressed in the following statements:

"THE SPIRIT WITH OUR SPIRIT"
The Secret of God's Organic Salvation

1) The generating Spirit in our spirit, quickened by Christ, regenerates us, giving us authority to be the children of God, begotten of God.

2) The nourishing Spirit in our spirit, cherished by Christ, feeds us with the spiritual milk of the Word that we may grow unto salvation.

3) The sanctifying Spirit from our spirit, captivated by Christ, sanctifies us with the nature of God, making us holy unto God.

4) The renewing Spirit in our spirit, indwelt by Christ, renews us that we may put on the new man through the breaking of the cross.

5) The transforming Spirit in our spirit, filled by Christ, transforms us into the glorious image of Christ for His expression.

6) The building Spirit in our spirit, possessed by Christ, builds us into the house of God and the Body of Christ for Their dwelling.

7) The maturing Spirit in our spirit, enriched with Christ, conforms us to the image of Christ, the firstborn Son of God—the model of God's sons.

8) The sealing Spirit in our spirit, exulting with Christ,

saturates us with and brings us into the glory of God for our glorification.

The Secret of God's Intensified Salvation

9) The intensified Spirit in our spirit, drawn by the Lamb, motivates us to overcome the degradation of the church for the Body of Christ to consummate the New Jerusalem.

All these points involve the Spirit with our spirit. Here the term *the Spirit* does not refer merely to the Spirit of God but to the consummated Spirit—the Spirit who has passed through the processes of incarnation, human living, crucifixion, and resurrection. This is the Spirit who, in John 7:39, was "not yet, because Jesus had not yet been glorified." After Christ was glorified in resurrection, He became the life-giving Spirit (1 Cor. 15:45b). This life-giving Spirit is *the Spirit,* that is, the consummated Spirit.

The Spirit of God has passed through a process, and our spirit also has passed through a process. Our spirit was created by God, but through Adam it became fallen and deadened. However, our deadened spirit was redeemed by Christ and, having been redeemed, it has been quickened, enlivened, by the Spirit, who regenerated us. The consummated Spirit is in our regenerated spirit. When we speak of the Spirit with our spirit, we mean that the consummated Spirit is with the believers' created and regenerated spirit. Now we need to see that the Spirit with our spirit is the secret of all the experiences of God's organic salvation: regeneration, feeding, sanctification, renewing, transformation, building, conformation, and glorification.

My burden in these messages is to present the best theology in eight sections concerning God's organic salvation plus one section concerning God's intensified salvation. The eight sections of God's organic salvation are regeneration, feeding, sanctification, renewing, transformation, building, conformation, and glorification. The additional section is intensification. These nine points cover much genuine theology. I believe that if you study these messages, which may be regarded as a theological lesson book, you will learn the best theology.

The title of this chapter is "The Secret of Regeneration." In these messages we are using the word *secret* as a noun meaning skillfulness in doing things or in making things. Paul used this word in Philippians 4:12: "I know also how to be abased, and I know how to abound; in everything and in all things I have learned the secret both to be filled and to hunger, both to abound and to lack." Paul had learned the secret, the skillfulness, of facing every kind of situation. The secret of these eight sections of God's organic salvation is the Spirit with our spirit. These two spirits working together is the skillfulness, the secret, of all spiritual things, especially of all the aspects of God's organic salvation.

I. THE DIVINE TRINITY'S SEEKING OF THE LOST SINNERS

Luke 15 unveils the seeking by the Triune God of the lost sinners. Man was created by God but became fallen, and now fallen men are lost sinners. However, in order to fulfill His desire for His good pleasure, God still loved the lost human race, and two thousand years ago the Triune God came to rescue the lost sinners.

A. The Second of the Divine Trinity Coming to Seek the Lost Sinners

The Second of the Divine Trinity, the Son, came to seek the lost sinners outside of them objectively as a shepherd seeks his lost sheep (Luke 15:4). This seeking was outside of the lost sinners and on the cross. John 10 proves that Christ's seeking is objective, outside of us, and on the cross. The Lord Jesus said, "I am the good Shepherd; the good Shepherd lays down His life for the sheep" (v. 11). It was through His death on the cross that the Lord Jesus laid down His life for us. This was His seeking us objectively on the cross.

B. The Third of the Divine Trinity Coming to Seek the Lost Sinners

Then the third of the Divine Trinity, the Spirit, comes to seek the lost sinners with the enlightening Word within them subjectively in their heart, as a woman seeking her lost coin by lighting a lamp (Luke 15:8). Whereas the Son's seeking is objective on the cross, the Spirit's seeking is subjective and within the sinner's heart. First, in the eyes of God we are the lost sheep, and, second, we are lost coins. We were lost and common, but the Triune God came to sanctify us from being common. This is the initial sanctification of the Spirit to separate a lost sinner from among all the others unto repentance to God for the receiving of Christ's redemption (1 Pet. 1:2; see Chapter Two, point II.A.1.). Here the word *unto* means "resulting in." The initial sanctification of the Spirit results in repentance.

II. THE SECRET OF REGENERATION

Let us now begin to consider the secret of regeneration.

A. The Spirit of Reality
Coming to Convict the Sinners

The Spirit of reality, who has sanctified the lost sinners unto repentance, comes to convict the lost sinners concerning three things: concerning sin, which is from Adam; concerning righteousness, which is of Christ; and concerning judgment, which belongs to Satan (John 16:8-11). Sin is from Adam. We all were born sinners in Adam, and thus we all are sinful. But God has a way to rescue us, and this rescue is a matter of righteousness, which is not only of Christ but which is Christ Himself. In Christ and by Christ God has rescued us from sin into righteousness. We were sinners, but through our believing into Christ, we have become righteous before God. Judgment is for Satan. Anyone who does not believe into Christ to be righteous will suffer Satan's judgment.

The Spirit's coming to convict concerning sin, righteousness, and judgment involves three persons—Adam, Christ, and Satan. Sin entered through Adam (Rom. 5:12), righteousness is the resurrected Christ (John 16:10; 1 Cor. 1:30), and judgment is for Satan (John 16:11), who is the author and source of sin (8:44). In Adam we were born of sin. The only way to be freed from sin is to believe into Christ, the Son of God (16:9). If we believe into Him, He becomes righteousness to us, and we are justified in Him (Rom. 3:24; 4:25). If we do not repent of the sin that is in Adam and believe into Christ, the Son of God, we will remain in sin and share the judgment of Satan for eternity (Matt. 25:41). These are the main points of the gospel. The Spirit uses these points to convict the lost sinners.

B. The Sinners Born Anew

John 3:3 and 5 tell us that regeneration is to be born anew. The Spirit convicts sinners that they may be born anew of water (the water of baptism signifying death) and of the Spirit (who has sanctified the sinners from among others and who is the reality of resurrection) in their spirit enlivened by Christ in resurrection. The water of baptism indicates that, if we would be regenerated, we must admit that we are good only to be put on the cross with Christ and buried. This means that we are finished and that our past, our history, is gone. Because the Spirit who sanctifies us is the reality of resurrection, when we have Him, we have resurrection. It is resurrection that regenerates us.

C. Through the Resurrection of Christ

Regeneration is through the resurrection of Christ that He may impart the divine life into the lost sinners as the authority for them to be the children of God, begotten of God as His species (1 Pet. 1:3; John 1:12-13). When Christ was resurrected, all His believers, chosen and given to Him by God, were included in Him. Hence, they were resurrected with Him (Eph. 2:6) and regenerated through Him that they may have the eternal life as the authority for them to be children of God as His species. Through regeneration we, who are human, have become God-men; we have become God's kind.

D. That Which Is Born of the Spirit

John 3:6b says, "That which is born of the Spirit is spirit." *The Spirit* is the Spirit of God, and *spirit* is the spirit of a sinner born anew.

E. A Great Washing

Such a regeneration, a new birth, is a great washing, purging the regenerated believer from the oldness of his old creation and reconditioning, remaking, remodeling, our old being in life (Titus 3:5; cf. Matt. 19:28). The Greek word for *regeneration* in Titus 3:5 is different from that for *regenerated* in 1 Peter 1:23. The only other place this word is used is in Matthew 19:28, where it is used for the restoration in the millennium. In Titus 3:5 it refers to a change from one state to another. Being born again is the commencing of this change. The washing of regeneration begins with our being born again and continues with the renewing of the Holy Spirit as the process of God's new creation, a process that makes us a new man. It is a kind of reconditioning, remaking, or remodeling, with life.

No matter how good we may be in ourselves, we are still an old creation. Only regeneration can wash away the oldness of this old creation. When we were regenerated, born anew, born of God, of the death water, we became new, and now regeneration is washing away all the oldness from our being as an old creation.

F. To Drink of the Life-giving Spirit

To be regenerated is to drink the life-giving Spirit (1 Cor. 12:13) as the living water. First Corinthians 12:13 says, "In one Spirit we were all baptized into one body...and were all given to drink one Spirit." The Pentecostal people talk much about the baptism of the Spirit but say little, if anything, about drinking the Spirit. To be baptized in water is one thing, but to drink the water is another thing. If we do not drink water, no water can get into us. We should not only be baptized in the Spirit but also drink the Spirit. God's way is to baptize us and then give us to drink. We need to drink the life-giving Spirit as the living water.

1. Living Water Given to the Believer

The Lord Jesus gives living water to the believer regenerated by Him (John 4:10; 7:37). When we were regenerated, He gave us water.

2. The River of Water of Life

The life-giving Spirit as the living water is the Spirit flowing as the river of water of life from the throne of the Triune God (Rev. 22:1, 17; 21:6). Actually, the flow of the Triune God is the living water which constitutes the river.

3. A Spring Gushing Up into Eternal Life

The living water which the Lord Jesus gives to a believer regenerated by Him becomes a spring of water gushing up into eternal life (John 4:14). We need to know the difference between the fountain and the spring. The fountain is the source. When water comes out of the fountain, the water becomes the spring. God is the fountain, the Spirit of Jesus is the spring, and we, the believers, are the ones in whom the spring is gushing up. All this is included in regeneration, because to be regenerated is to drink the life-giving Spirit.

G. By Exercising the Spirit

The experiences of the foregoing points (A through F) are all by exercising the spirit of a repentant and saved sinner through prayer to call on the name of the Lord (Eph. 6:18; Rom. 10:13). Just as we exercise our feet by walking, so we exercise our spirit by praying. According to Ephesians 6:18 every time we pray we should exercise our spirit. Furthermore, to pray is mainly to call on the name of the Lord.

H. Receiving the Word of God

The experiences of the foregoing points are also by receiving the living and abiding word of God (the word of the Spirit of life—John 6:63; 1 Pet. 1:23). First we need to exercise our spirit to contact the living Spirit, and then we need to receive the living and abiding word of God, the word of the Spirit of life.

I. Receiving the Spirit of Sonship

A saved one receives the Spirit of sonship in his spirit

(Gal. 4:5-6; Rom. 8:15). The Spirit we have received is the Spirit of sonship, and this Spirit makes us a son of God.

J. The Witnessing of the Spirit of God
with Our Spirit

The Spirit of God with our spirit witnesses that we, the regenerated believers, are the children of God (Rom. 8:16). First, the Spirit regenerates us in our spirit, and then He witnesses with our spirit that we, the regenerated ones, are the children of God.

K. The Sons of God

Romans 8:14 says, "As many as are led by the Spirit of God, these are sons of God." When we follow the leading of the Spirit in our daily living, this is an evidence that we are a son of God.

L. A Part of the Bride
as the Increase of Christ

A regenerated believer in Christ is a part of the bride as the increase of Christ the Bridegroom (John 3:3, 5-6, 29-30). The regenerated believers in Christ are not part of a company going to heaven; they are a part of the bride of Christ. Many preach the gospel by quoting the word in John 3 about being born again, but not many connect the word concerning regeneration in the first part of John 3 with the word concerning the bride in the last part of this chapter. John 3:29a says, "He who has the bride is the bridegroom," and verse 30a says, "He must increase." The increase in verse 30 is the bride in verse 29, and the bride is a composition of all the regenerated believers. According to the context, therefore, all the regenerated persons are parts of the bride, and the bride is the increase of the Bridegroom, just as Eve was the increase of Adam.

M. Learning to Worship God

Every child of God should learn to worship God, who is Spirit, with his regenerated spirit mingled with God's Spirit as one spirit (John 4:24; 1 Cor. 6:17).

N. Needing to Serve God

A child of God should also serve God with his spirit in the gospel (Rom. 1:9; 12:11). We should both worship God and serve God in our regenerated spirit.

CHAPTER TWO

THE SECRET OF FEEDING
AND SANCTIFICATION

OUTLINE

I. The secret of feeding (the continuation of regeneration)—the second section of God's organic salvation:
  A. The initial feeding:
    1. To feed the newborn babes—new believers.
    2. Through the cherishing of them to pray-read the word and call on the Lord by exercising their spirit cherished by Christ.
    3. With the milk of the word, which is the Spirit— John 6:63; Eph. 6:17.
    4. For their growth in the divine life unto their daily salvation—1 Pet. 2:2.
  B. The continual feeding:
    1. To feed the growing believers.
    2. With the solid word, which is the Spirit of life—Heb. 5:14.
    3. For their maturity in the divine life unto transformation and conformation to the image of Christ.
  C. Feeding in shepherding:
    1. Christ as the One who came that the believers may have life (John 10:10b) is the good Shepherd giving His life for redeeming the believers and rising up to feed His sheep with Himself as the green pasture that they may have life more abundantly (vv. 2-4, 9, 11, 14-16).
    2. He shepherds all His believers and guides them to springs of waters of life—Rev. 7:17.

3. He as the great Shepherd shepherds God's flock in resurrection for their perfection to do God's will within them—Heb. 13:20-21.

4. He is the Shepherd of the believers' soul within the believers to oversee them—1 Pet. 2:25.

5. He is the Chief Shepherd who will reward the faithful elders, who shepherd God's flock faithfully, with the unfading crown of glory for their encouragement—1 Pet. 5:4.

6. He commissioned Peter, the apostle appointed by Him, to feed His lambs and shepherd His sheep in his loving of Him— John 21:15-17.

7. He as the Head gives the Body gifted persons, one kind of which are the shepherds, who perfect the saints by teaching for the building up of the Body of Christ—Eph. 4:11-12.

8. The main responsibility of the elders in the church is to shepherd God's flock by teaching faithfully—1 Pet. 5:2-3; 1 Tim. 3:2; 5:17.

9. The elders' shepherding of the church, the flock of God, is the best way to take care of the "fierce wolves" and those speaking perverted things among the churches—Acts 20:28-30.

II. The secret of sanctification—the third section of God's organic salvation:

A. God's sanctification of the believers is of three aspects:

1. The first aspect is the seeking sanctification by the Holy Spirit with the enlightening word initially—1 Pet. 1:2; Luke 15:8.

2. The second aspect is the positional sanctification by the redeeming blood of Christ judicially—Heb. 13:12; 10:29.

3. The third aspect is the dispositional sanctification by the Holy Spirit organically—Rom. 15:16; 6:19, 22.

B. We are created by God in the particular sense that we are for Him. But we became fallen from God, and we were lost in our position (standing) and in our nature (disposition), becoming common. Hence, in saving us, God sanctified us both in our position, in our standing before Him, outwardly and judicially, and in our fallen disposition inwardly and organically. We have covered God's positional and judicial sanctification on other occasions. What is covered in this message is God's dispositional and organic sanctification:

1. By the Holy Spirit—Rom. 15:16:
   a. In their disposition.
   b. With the divine, holy nature of God (2 Pet. 1:4) that they may be holy unto God (Eph. 1:4).
   c. With the element of the resurrection life of Christ, which they received through the feeding.
2. From their spirit captivated by Christ, through their soul, and unto their body, so that their entire being can be wholly sanctified—1 Thes. 5:23.

C. Since all the believers will be the components of the holy city, New Jerusalem, all of them should be sanctified to be as holy as the HOLY CITY, the New Jerusalem.

Prayer: Lord, we extol You as the speaking God. You spoke in ancient times, and we have Your Word in our hand. Lord, You are still speaking as the Spirit. Your Spirit is the speaking Spirit, and we listen to His speaking. Lord, You are speaking through Your Son, and we are a part of Your sonship. We believe You are still speaking through us. Thank You, Lord, for Your speaking. In the past seventy-four years in Your recovery Your speaking has not ceased. Every year You have given us new light and new revelation by Your speaking. How we thank You! In the last few years Your speaking among us has been very much enriched. Lord, we ask You once again to release what You have shown us. Lord, bless it and use it. We know that Your intention is to build up the Body of Your Son, which is the organism of the Triune God. Lord, we can do nothing. We trust in You. Amen.

In the previous chapter we pointed out that the word *secret* denotes the skillful way of doing things. The secret of God's organic salvation is the Spirit with our spirit. This Spirit is the generating Spirit, the nourishing Spirit, the sanctifying Spirit, the renewing Spirit, the transforming Spirit, the building Spirit, the maturing Spirit, the sealing Spirit, and the intensified Spirit. Have you ever realized that the Spirit has these nine aspects? Our spirit needs to be touched by Christ in nine ways and become a spirit quickened by Christ, cherished by Christ, captivated by Christ, indwelt by Christ, filled by Christ, possessed by Christ, enriched with Christ, exulting with Christ, and drawn by the Lamb. Is your spirit in these nine states? Your spirit has been quickened by Christ, but has it been cherished by Christ and captivated by Christ? If your spirit has been captivated by Christ, then you must be like the one in the Song of Songs, one who has been captivated by Christ, the captivating One. Your spirit is surely indwelt by Christ, and now the renewing Spirit is doing a renewing work within you. In order to renew us, Christ as the Spirit must dwell in our spirit. Your spirit should also be filled by Christ so that you can be transformed and then built up with others. If you would be built up with others in the Body of Christ, your spirit needs to be possessed by Christ. Building is impossible if we are not possessed by Christ in our spirit.

You also need to be enriched by Christ in your spirit. If your spirit is enriched with Christ, you will be able to mature. Furthermore, your spirit needs to be in a state of exulting with Christ. This exulting is related to your being saturated with the glory of God and being brought into the glory of God for your glorification. Surely we all will exult at the time of Christ's coming and of our rapture and the transfiguration of our body to be "conformed to the body of His glory" (Phil. 3:21). Finally, your spirit should be drawn by the Lamb. The overcomers in Revelation 14 are drawn by the Christ as the Lamb and follow Him wherever He may go (v. 4).

In this message we will cover two sections of God's organic salvation—the section of feeding and the section of sanctification. These sections are closely related, for without feeding there can be no sanctification. Sanctification is by feeding. The more we feed on the word of God, the more we are sanctified. The word on which we feed sanctifies us. In John 17:17 the Lord Jesus prayed, "Sanctify them in the truth; Your word is truth." The word contains the element with which God sanctifies us. For this reason, feeding and sanctification are closely related.

I. THE SECRET OF FEEDING

Feeding is the second section of God's organic salvation. In God's organic salvation feeding is the continuation of regeneration. As all mothers know, after a baby has been delivered the baby needs feeding. Mothers also know that the best way to comfort and satisfy a baby is to nurse him, feeding him with milk. Feeding is, therefore, the continuation of birth, of regeneration.

Regeneration brings us into a divine existence and makes us divine persons. As the continuation of regeneration, feeding enables us to maintain and develop our divine existence. Feeding is an ongoing process that will continue through all the following sections of God's organic salvation—sanctification, renewing, transformation, building up, conformation, and glorification. Feeding, therefore, will continue all the way from regeneration to glorification. If we see this, we will not look down on the matter of feeding. It is by feeding that we receive the element with which God sanctifies us, and it is by feeding that we receive the riches with which God renews us, transforms us, builds us up, conforms us, and glorifies us.

A. The Initial Feeding

The initial feeding is to feed the newborn babes, the new believers. We feed them through cherishing them to pray-read the word and call on the Lord by exercising their spirit cherished by Christ. As a mother feeds her child, she will often try to make the child happy, cherishing him. After she cherishes the child, she gives him something to eat, and the child will eat. We all need to be cherished. When we are cherished by Christ, we are happy to take the word. We should cherish the new believers to pray-read the word by exercising their spirit. If the new believers are cherished, they will be willing to exercise their spirit to pray-read the word.

Whenever we pray, we should pray in the spirit (Eph. 6:18). We exercise our feet by walking, and we exercise our spirit by praying. When we are cherished by Christ, first we feel happy, and then spontaneously we exercise our spirit to pray, calling on the Lord. It is very difficult to pray without calling on the Lord. Romans 10:12 says that the Lord is "rich to all who call upon Him." When we call on the Lord, we enjoy His riches.

We feed the newborn babes, the new believers, with the milk of the word, which is the Spirit (John 6:63; Eph. 6:17), for their growth in the divine life unto their daily salvation (1 Pet. 2:2). In John 6:63 the Lord Jesus says, "The words which I have spoken to you are spirit and are life." The fact that the word is life implies that it contains nourishing milk. According to 1 Peter 2 we feed on the milk of the word in order to "grow unto salvation." This salvation is not the eternal salvation, which we have already, but the daily salvation.

Because we have eternal salvation, we will not perish. However, we may be defeated every day and become a failure, for example in losing our temper with our spouse. In Philippians 2:14 Paul charges us to do "all things without murmurings and reasonings." Reasonings are of our mind and come mainly from the brothers, whereas murmurings are of the emotion and come mainly from the sisters. We need to be saved daily from murmurings and reasonings. To be saved in this way is to work out our own salvation according to God's operating in us.

We need to be saved daily from many different things. For instance, a certain brother may be a quick person. As such a person, he always does things in a quick way. This may be good most of the time, but it is not good all of the time. Spiritually speaking, it is not good to act quickly, because when we are too quick in doing things, it indicates that we are doing things by ourselves without trusting in the Lord. Whenever we do things by trusting in the Lord, we will slow down and even stop. For a brother to be saved from his quickness is a matter of daily salvation.

B. The Continual Feeding

The initial feeding is followed by the continual feeding. The continual feeding is to feed the growing believers with the solid word, which is the Spirit of life (Heb. 5:14), for their maturity in the divine life unto transformation and conformation to the image of Christ. At first, a mother feeds her baby with milk, but as the child grows she feeds him with solid food. The principle is the same in feeding the growing believers. Certain portions of the Bible are solid food. For example, the word concerning the New Jerusalem in Revelation 21 and 22 is not milk but solid food. If we only drink milk, we cannot mature. In order to mature, we need solid food.

C. Feeding in Shepherding

The feeding in God's organic salvation also includes the feeding in shepherding. In John 21:15 the Lord Jesus charged Peter, saying, "Feed My lambs." In verse 16 He said to him, "Shepherd My sheep," and in verse 17 He went on to say, "Feed My sheep." If we do not know how to shepherd, we will not be able to feed others. The main purpose of the small groups and the vital groups in the church life is not merely to take care of one another but to shepherd one another. You shepherd me, and I shepherd you. You are a sheep under my shepherding, and I am a sheep under your shepherding. This is mutual shepherding. In shepherding others, we should first cherish them in order to make them happy, and then we should feed them. This kind of feeding is the real shepherding.

Shepherding implies teaching. This is indicated in Ephesians 4:11, which says that the Head has given to the Body "some as apostles and some as prophets and some as evangelists and some as shepherds and teachers." This verse does not say "some as shepherds and some as teachers." Rather, this verse says "some as shepherds and teachers," indicating that they are the same persons in a single category. Therefore, teaching and shepherding go together.

1. The Good Shepherd

Christ as the One who came that the believers may have life (John 10:10b) is the good Shepherd giving His life for redeeming the believers and rising up to feed His sheep with Himself as the green pasture that they may have life more abundantly (vv. 2-4, 9, 11, 14-16). In John 14:16 the Lord Jesus said, "I will ask the Father, and He will give you another Comforter." This other Comforter is the Spirit. The Lord was the first Shepherd, and the Spirit, the second Comforter as His continuation, is also a Shepherd.

2. Shepherding All His Believers

Christ shepherds all His believers and guides them to springs of waters of life (Rev. 7:17). In eternity future Christ will be our eternal Shepherd guiding us to springs of waters of life.

3. The Great Shepherd

Christ as the great Shepherd shepherds God's flock in resurrection for their perfection to do God's will within them (Heb. 13:20-21). The believers can do God's will within them by being perfected through the shepherding of Christ in resurrection. Today Christ is in resurrection, and He is shepherding us from within. When He shepherds us in this way, we do God's will.

4. The Shepherd of the Believers' Soul

Christ within the believers is the Shepherd of the believers' soul to oversee them (1 Pet. 2:25). He is our Shepherd not only outwardly but also inwardly. He shepherds us from within, in our being, in our soul, to oversee us. Our soul needs Christ's shepherding with His observation, oversight, and correction so that we may be strengthened. This kind of shepherding also involves feeding. Our soul needs Christ's shepherding with His feeding.

5. The Chief Shepherd

Christ is the Chief Shepherd who will reward the faithful elders, who shepherd God's flock faithfully, with the unfading crown of glory for their encouragement (1 Pet. 5:4). Christ Himself is the Shepherd, and He has established elders in the churches and has charged them to shepherd "the flock of God" (v. 2).

The first responsibility of the elders is to shepherd God's flock, the church, not to take care of business affairs. The elders should leave the business affairs to the deacons, the serving ones, and devote more time to shepherding. However, in most of the churches the elders are doing the deacons' work and are neglecting the matter of shepherding. If the elders do not trust the deacons to care for the business affairs, including bookkeeping, the elders will not have time to shepherd the saints. I would urge every elder to visit at least one saint every day. Without the elders' shepherding, the church cannot be built up. All the believers, regardless of their stage of spiritual growth, need shepherding. Even a brief word spoken to a saint after a meeting will comfort, encourage, and strengthen that one.

I would encourage all the elders to contact the saints one by one over a period of a few months. If the elders are faithful to do this, the church will be reconditioned. The elders' shepherding will recondition the church.

6. The Lord's Commission to Peter

Because the church needs shepherding, the Lord Jesus commissioned Peter, the apostle appointed by Him, to shepherd His lambs and feed His sheep in his loving of Him (John 21:15-17). As we have pointed out, the Lord charged him to feed His lambs, to shepherd His sheep, and to feed His sheep. Today we need to feed the lambs, the younger ones, and to shepherd the older ones.

7. The Gifted Persons

Christ as the Head gives the Body gifted persons, one kind of which are the shepherds, who perfect the saints by teaching for the building up of the Body of Christ (Eph. 4:11-12). Shepherding is very important for the building up of the Body of Christ.

8. The Main Responsibility of the Elders

The main responsibility of the elders in the church is to shepherd God's flock by teaching faithfully (1 Pet. 5:2-3; 1 Tim. 3:2; 5:17). An elder should be apt to teach (1 Tim. 3:2). The words *apt to teach* indicate that the elders should have the heart, the desire, and the habit to teach. This is a qualification for one to be an elder. In 1 Timothy 5:17 Paul says that "those who labor in word and teaching" should be counted worthy of double honor. The elders should labor not in the business affairs but in word and teaching, shepherding God's flock by teaching faithfully.

9. The Elders' Shepherding of the Flock of God Being the Best Way to Take Care of the "Fierce Wolves"

The elders' shepherding of the church, the flock of God, is the best way to take care of the "fierce wolves" and those speaking perverted things among the churches (Acts 20:28-30). Often elders have asked me what they should do about those in the church who speak perverted things. The way for the elders to deal with such a situation is to shepherd the church. Many years of history have proved that the elders' shepherding will keep the saints from the "fierce wolves" and from those who speak perverted things.

II. THE SECRET OF SANCTIFICATION

Sanctification is the third section of God's organic salvation.

A. The Three Aspects of God's Sanctification

God's sanctification of the believers is of three aspects.

1. The First Aspect

The first aspect is the seeking sanctification by the Holy Spirit with the enlightening Word initially (1 Pet. 1:2; Luke 15:8). First Peter 1:2 speaks of "the sanctification of the Spirit unto the obedience and sprinkling of the blood of Jesus Christ." Here we have initial sanctification—the sanctification of the Spirit that comes before obedience to Christ and faith in His redemption, that is, before justification through Christ's redemption (Rom. 3:24). This aspect of sanctification is seen also in Luke 15:8. In Luke 15, a chapter on the salvation of the Triune God, the Son (the shepherd) seeks the lost sinner objectively, and the Spirit (the woman) seeks the lost sinner subjectively by working within the repenting sinner. In verse 8 the seeking Spirit is likened to a woman who lit a lamp, swept the house, and sought carefully until she found the lost coin. This signifies the initial sanctification by the Holy Spirit.

2. The Second Aspect

The second aspect is the positional sanctification by the redeeming blood of Christ judicially (Heb. 13:12; 10:29).

3. The Third Aspect

The third aspect is the dispositional sanctification by the Holy Spirit organically (Rom. 15:16; 6:19, 22). Regarding the three aspects of God's sanctification we need to remember three words: *initially, judicially,* and *organically.*

B. In Our Position and in Our Disposition

We are created by God in the particular sense that we are for Him. But we became fallen from God, and we were lost in our position (standing) and in our nature (disposition), becoming common, a very serious matter. Hence, in saving us, God sanctified us both in our position, in our standing before Him, outwardly and judicially, and in our fallen disposition inwardly and organically. We have covered God's positional and judicial sanctification on other occasions. What is covered in this message is God's dispositional and organic sanctification.

1. By the Holy Spirit

Dispositional sanctification is by the Holy Spirit (Rom. 15:16). God's positional sanctification is to sanctify our outward standing before Him by the redeeming blood of Christ judicially; whereas God's dispositional sanctification is to sanctify our inward fallen nature by the Spirit organically through our spirit captivated by Christ.

a. In Our Disposition

The Spirit sanctifies the believers in their disposition. The word *disposition* refers to nature. The word *nature* refers to the substance created by God. *Disposition,* a negative word, denotes our distorted and crooked nature. The nature, the natural substance, created by God was good, but in us, the fallen people, nature has become disposition—our distorted, crooked, perverted nature. Therefore, when referring to our fallen nature, we use the negative word *disposition.*

b. With the Nature of God

In God's organic salvation we are being sanctified in our disposition with the divine, holy nature of God (2 Pet. 1:4) that we may be holy unto God. God has chosen us to be holy (Eph. 1:4). For us to be holy means that we possess and partake of God's holy nature and participate in God's divinity.

c. With the Element of the Resurrection Life of Christ

The Holy Spirit is sanctifying us also with the element of the resurrection life of Christ, which we received through the feeding. The more we feed on the Word, the more we receive the element of the resurrection life of Christ for our dispositional sanctification.

2. Wholly Sanctified

The believers are being sanctified from their spirit, through their soul, and unto their body, so that their entire being can be wholly sanctified. First Thessalonians 5:23 indicates that sanctification begins from our spirit, spreads through our soul, and consummates with the sanctification of our body. In this way our whole being will be sanctified.

C. To Be as Holy as the Holy City, New Jerusalem

Since all the believers will be the components of the holy city, New Jerusalem, all of them should be sanctified to be as holy as the holy city, the New Jerusalem. Unless we are made holy, we will not be qualified to be a part of the holy city, the New Jerusalem. As the holy city, the New Jerusalem is composed of holy believers.

CHAPTER THREE

THE SECRET OF RENEWING AND TRANSFORMATION

OUTLINE

I. The secret of renewing—the fourth section of God's organic salvation:

    A. All the regenerated believers have been created into one new man in Christ (Eph. 2:15; Col. 3:10); hence, they are God's new creation (2 Cor. 5:17; Gal. 6:15).

    B. But this new creation is out of God's old creation, of which so many old things should be renewed to become new.

    C. In fact, the creation of the new man has been completed by Christ on the cross (Eph. 2:15); but in practicality, the believers, who are the members of the new man, should apply to themselves what Christ has completed by being practically renewed in their living.

    D. Renewing is implied in sanctification, which makes the believers new while it is going on within them.

    E. Renewing is the continuation of the washing of regeneration—Titus 3:5.

    F. The means of renewing:

        1. By the renewing Spirit (Titus 3:5) mingling with the believers' regenerated spirit indwelt by Christ as one spirit to spread into the believers' mind (Eph. 4:23) to renew their entire being as a member of the new man.

        2. By the believers' walking in the newness of the divine life in resurrection—Rom. 6:4:

      a. Putting off the old man, that is, by renouncing and denying their old self (Matt. 16:24)—Eph. 4:22.

      b. Putting on the new man, that is, by applying what Christ has accomplished in creating the new man, by living and magnifying Christ through the bountiful supply of the Spirit of Jesus Christ—Eph. 4:24; Phil. 1:19-21.

G. Renewing is through the consuming by the believers' environmental suffering—2 Cor. 4:16:

  1. Killing their outer man.

  2. Renewing their inner man day by day.

H. The believers must be thoroughly and absolutely renewed that they may be practically the genuine new creation of God and for God—Gal. 6:15.

I. The believers should be renewed to be as new as the New Jerusalem since they all will be the consummating part of the New Jerusalem—Rev. 21:2.

II. The secret of transformation—the fifth section of God's organic salvation:

A. Regeneration has added the divine life to the believers' redeemed life, making the two a "grafted" life; thus, the believers participate in God's divinity.

B. Sanctification has sanctified the believers, especially in their nature, with the holy nature of God to change their nature; thus, they also participate in God's divinity.

C. Renewing has renewed the believers mainly in their mind to change their mind with the mind of Christ; thus, they also participate in God's divinity.

D. Transformation transforms the believers' entire being, by the transforming Spirit in their spirit filled with Christ, into the glorious image of Christ, that they may fully participate in God's divinity:

1. It is by renewing (Rom. 12:2b); it is the issue of renewing.
2. Renewing is mainly in the believers' mind (Eph. 4:23); transformation is in the believers' soul for their entire being.
3. It is not any kind of outward correction or adjustment.
4. It is a kind of metabolism, by the addition of the element of the divine life of Christ into their being, to be expressed outwardly in the image of Christ.
5. It is accomplished by the Lord Spirit (the pneumatic Christ), transforming the believers into the image of the glory of Christ—2 Cor. 3:18.
6. The believers should behold the Lord with an unveiled face and reflect Him like a mirror to express Him.
7. The believers should live and walk by the Spirit (Gal. 5:16, 25) and walk according to the mingled spirit (Rom. 8:4b), that the divine life of Christ may have the way to regulate them and transform them into the image of the Lord in glory.
8. Transformation should be consummated by conformation, which is maturity in the divine life for the believers to be conformed to the image of Christ, the firstborn Son of God; thus, they manifest God in life, in nature, in inward thinking, and in outward expression.

Prayer: Lord, we extol You with our full acknowledgment. We acknowledge that You are the Lord of all, that You are the speaking God, and that You are the Spirit who dispenses Your life into our being. Lord, we praise You that we can acknowledge so many things concerning You. Lord, in speaking Your word, we pray that You will be one spirit with us and that You will speak in our speaking, making our speaking Your speaking. Lord, we want to be one spirit with You. We do not want to do anything or to speak anything without being one spirit with You. Lord, in these days, You are teaching us to speak the things of a new culture in a new language. Lord, we ask You to give us the new language for the new culture. Amen.

In this message we come to the next two sections of God's organic salvation—renewing and transformation.

I. THE SECRET OF RENEWING

Renewing is the fourth section of God's organic salvation.

A. One New Man

All the regenerated believers have been created into one new man in Christ (Eph. 2:15; Col. 3:10); hence, they are God's new creation (2 Cor. 5:17; Gal. 6:15). In Christ we, both the Jewish believers and the Gentile believers, have been created into the new man.

B. The New Creation

This new creation is out of God's old creation, of which so many old things should be renewed to become new. We may regard ourselves as quite good, but whether we are good or bad, we are of the old creation, and thus we need to be renewed.

C. The Creation of the New Man

In fact, the creation of the new man has been completed by Christ on the cross (Eph. 2:15); but in practicality, the believers, who are the members of the new man, should apply to themselves what Christ has completed by being practically renewed in their living. We need to apply to ourselves what Christ has accomplished.

D. Renewing Implied in Sanctification

Renewing is implied in sanctification, which makes the believers new while it is going on within them. The more we are sanctified, the more we are renewed. To be renewed, therefore, is based on the ongoing sanctification.

E. The Continuation of the Washing of Regeneration

Titus 3:5 says that God "saved us, through the washing of regeneration and the renewing of the Holy Spirit." This tells us that renewing is the continuation of the washing of regeneration. God first regenerates us and then continues to renew us. Regeneration lays the foundation of the divine life upon which the renewing continues to build up the divine life within a believer. Regeneration is accomplished once for all, but renewing is an ongoing process through the whole life of a believer until he becomes matured to be a full-grown man.

In regeneration a new life, the divine life, is added to our natural life, causing these two lives to become one. In sanctification our distorted, crooked, and perverted nature is adjusted by God's holy nature. In renewing the mingled spirit penetrates our troublesome mind, causing it to be changed and even to become the mind of Christ (Phil. 2:5; 1 Cor. 2:16). Our mind is the source of all kinds of trouble and surely needs to be renewed.

F. The Means of Renewing

1. By the Renewing Spirit

We are renewed by the Spirit (Titus 3:5). Renewing is by the renewing Spirit mingling with the believers' regenerated spirit indwelt by Christ as one spirit to spread into the believers' mind (Eph. 4:23) to renew their entire being as a member of the new man.

2. By the Believers' Walking in the Newness of Life

We, the regenerated saints, as parts of the new man and as God's new creation should walk in the newness of the divine life in resurrection (Rom. 6:4).

a. Putting Off the Old Man

In order to be renewed by the mingled spirit, the renewing Spirit mingled with the believers' regenerated spirit, the believers need to put off their old man, that is, renounce and deny their old self (Eph. 4:22; Matt. 16:24). To deny the self and bear the cross is to apply the cross to the self.

b. Putting On the New Man

The believers also need to put on the new man, that is, apply what Christ has accomplished in creating the new man, by living and magnifying Christ through the bountiful supply of the Spirit of Jesus Christ (Eph. 4:24; Phil. 1:19-21). Whereas the cross is for the putting off of our old man, the Spirit is for the putting on of the new man. To put on the new man we need the bountiful supply of the Spirit of Jesus Christ.

G. Through Consuming

Renewing takes place through the consuming by the believers' environmental suffering (2 Cor. 4:16). This suffering kills the believers' outer man and renews their inner man day by day. Human life is more a life of suffering than a life of enjoyment. Much of the believers' environmental suffering is related to their family life, to their daily life with their spouse, children, and relatives. Our environment is according to God's sovereign arrangement, and we cannot escape it. God arranges our environment so that little by little and day by day our outer man will be consumed and our inner man will be renewed.

H. The Believers Needing to Be Renewed

The believers must be thoroughly and absolutely renewed that they may be practically the genuine new creation of God and for God (Gal. 6:15).

I. To Be as New as the New Jerusalem

The believers should be renewed to be as new as the New Jerusalem since they all will be the consummating part of the New Jerusalem (Rev. 21:2). Nothing of the old creation can be brought into the New Jerusalem. Since the New

Jerusalem will be constituted with the believers, they need to be thoroughly and absolutely renewed.

II. THE SECRET OF TRANSFORMATION

Transformation is the fifth section of God's organic salvation.

A. The Divine Life Added
to the Believers' Redeemed Life

Regeneration has added the divine life to the believers' redeemed life, making the two a "grafted" life; thus, the believers participate in God's divinity.

Some Christian teachers hold strongly to the concept of what is called an "exchanged life." This concept is found in the biography of J. Hudson Taylor written by his son and daughter-in-law. According to this concept, the Christian life is an exchanged life, a life in which we exchange our life for the divine life, the life of Christ. This teaching concerning an exchanged life is a great error. In the New Testament there is no such thing as an exchanged life. Yes, the first part of Galatians 2:20 says, "I am crucified with Christ; and it is no longer I who live." This, of course, is true: the old "I" has been crucified with Christ, and this "I" lives no longer. However, in this verse Paul goes on to say, "The life which I now live in the flesh I live in faith, the faith in the Son of God." On the one hand, the old "I" has been crucified; on the other hand, there is a new "I," and this new "I" lives by the faith of Christ. This is a matter not of an exchanged life but of a grafted life, two lives that have been grafted together to be one life. God has added His divine life to our redeemed human natural life and grafted our life with His life.

By means of this grafted life the believers participate in God's divinity. The believers are being mingled with God, and God is mingling Himself with them. As a result, the believers have divinity in their being and participate in God's divinity.

B. The Believers Sanctified
in Their Nature with the Nature of God

Sanctification has sanctified the believers, especially in

their nature, with the holy nature of God to change their nature; thus, they also participate in God's divinity. The more we are sanctified, the more we participate in God's divinity.

C. The Believers Renewed Mainly in Their Mind

Renewing has renewed the believers mainly in their mind to change their mind with the mind of Christ; thus, they also participate in God's divinity.

Three things cause us to participate in God's divinity: regeneration, sanctification, and renewing. Regeneration changes our life, sanctification changes our nature, and renewing changes our mind. All three things enable the believers in Christ to participate in God's divinity. If we realize this, we will see that as believers we are not only human but also divine. Today we, the believers in Christ, are both divine and human. We are human and divine persons. Because we are divine as well as human, we are also mystical.

D. The Believers' Entire Being Transformed

Transformation transforms the believers' entire being, by the transforming Spirit in their spirit filled with Christ, into the glorious image of Christ, that they may fully participate in God's divinity. To be filled with Christ, who is divine, is to be filled with divinity. At present we are participating in God's divinity only partially, but when our entire being is transformed and filled with divinity, we will fully participate in God's divinity.

1. The Issue of Renewing

Transformation is by renewing; it is the issue of renewing. Romans 12:2 says, "Do not be fashioned according to this age, but be transformed by the renewing of the mind." This indicates that transformation is the issue of renewing.

2. Transformation in the Believers' Soul

Renewing is mainly in the believers' mind (Eph. 4:23); transformation is in the believers' soul for their entire being.

3. Not Outward Correction or Adjustment

Transformation is not any kind of outward correction or adjustment.

4. A Kind of Metabolism

Transformation is a kind of metabolism, by the addition of the element of the divine life of Christ into the believers' being, to be expressed outwardly in the image of Christ. This can be illustrated by having a healthy complexion through proper nutrition. The way to have such a healthy complexion is not to apply cosmetics but to eat nourishing food and then to digest and assimilate it metabolically. If we eat properly, the food we digest and assimilate will supply us with a new element which will eventually produce an outward and visible change in our facial color. The principle is the same with transformation. Transformation is a matter of inward metabolism issuing in an outward expression.

5. By the Lord Spirit

Transformation is accomplished by the Lord Spirit (the pneumatic Christ), transforming the believers into the image of the glory of Christ (2 Cor. 3:18). The metabolism involved in transformation eventually transforms us into the image of the glory of Christ.

6. To Behold the Lord with an Unveiled Face

The believers should behold the Lord with an unveiled face and reflect Him like a mirror to express Him. This gives the ground and the way for the transforming Spirit to transform the believers' entire being into the glorious image of Christ as the firstborn Son of God who expresses God to the uttermost.

7. To Live and Walk by the Spirit

The believers should live and walk by the Spirit (Gal. 5:16, 25) and walk according to the mingled spirit (Rom. 8:4b), that the divine life of Christ may have the way to regulate them and transform them into the image of the Lord in glory.

8. *To Be Consummated by Conformation*

Transformation should be consummated by conformation, which is maturity in the divine life for the believers to be conformed to the image of Christ, the firstborn Son of God, to fully participate in God's divinity. Thus, they manifest God in life, in nature, in inward thinking, and in outward expression to enjoy the divine sonship and to participate in God's divinity in full.

At this point I would like to say a further word about a new utterance which the Lord has given us: *participate in God's divinity*. This language is very strange and marvelous. I believe that this word about participating in God's divinity is something altogether new. In God's organic salvation we, the believers in Christ, can participate in God's divinity. God's life has been imparted into our life, His nature is being wrought into our nature, His mind is being wrought into our mind, and we even have His divine element, the element of the riches of His unsearchable life, to transform our entire being. Thus, we have God's life, God's nature, God's mind, and the divine element of all His riches, and now we can participate in God's divinity in full. For us to participate in God's divinity means that He is making us Him. He is making us God in His life, in His nature, in His thinking, and in His expression but not, of course, in His Godhead.

For God to work Himself into us in such a way is not merely to make us holy, and it is not merely to make us perfect, victorious, and spiritual. God is working His life, nature, mind, and element into us in order to make us God in life, in nature, in mind, and in expression.

Regarding this, I have a very heavy burden for you all, especially for the co-workers and elders. I have the full assurance that you are one with the ministry for the Lord's recovery, and I appreciate this. However, I am very concerned that you may not realize and acknowledge that God has imparted His life into us, that He is working His nature into our nature, that He is working His mind into our mind, and that He is working the element of His unsearchable riches into our entire being, especially into our spirit and our soul.

Eventually, when our body is glorified, we will be the same as God in every part of our being. This is not a human thought—it is the divine revelation. We all need to see this and we all need to pray, "Lord, work Yourself into me richly in every aspect—in the aspects of Your life, Your nature, Your mind, and Your rich element—to make my whole being, spirit, soul, and body, the same as You are."

CHAPTER FOUR

THE SECRET OF BUILDING

OUTLINE

I. Something critical to the accomplishment of God's eternal economy:

   A. To be built up with the fellow believers is the Lord's supreme and highest requirement to His faithful seekers according to one of the divine attributes, the divine oneness, of the Divine Trinity—John 17.

   B. Being built up with the fellow partakers of the divine life is the highest virtue of the one who pursues after Christ in God's eternal economy.

   C. Not one of the descendants of the fallen adamic race has the capacity and ability to meet the high requirements of the kingdom of the heavens.

   D. Only the regenerated, sanctified, renewed, and transformed believers are qualified to fulfill the supreme requirements of the kingdom of the heavens.

   E. The God-men, who have the divine life, the divine nature, and the divine mind, and who participate in the divinity of God, have the divine capacity to carry out the divine requirements of the divine kingdom.

II. The secret of building—the sixth section of God's organic salvation:

   A. The prerequisites of the believers' building up in the church, the Body of Christ:

      1. To realize that the Lord loves and wants to

have a built church, not scattered individual believers.

2. To acknowledge that all the believers have been baptized in one Spirit into one Body and that God has placed the members in the Body and blended all the Body together—1 Cor. 12:13a, 18, 24.

3. To be in harmony with the fellow believers and to be in one accord with the Body in prayer, which issues in the establishment of the church— Matt. 18:19; Acts 1:14.

4. To practice the oneness of the Divine Trinity in the Divine Trinity as the Divine Trinity does— John 17:21-23:

   a. By the divine life with its source, the divine name of the Father—vv. 2-3, 6, 26.

   b. By the divine word as the truth that sanctifies the believers from the world— vv. 14-19.

   c. By the divine glory—the divine sonship with the Father's life and nature as the divine right to express the Father—vv. 22, 24.

5. To keep the oneness of the Spirit diligently— Eph. 4:3:

   a. In the constitution of the Body with the Divine Trinity as the source, the element, and the essence—vv. 4-6.

   b. Through the perfection by the gifted members for the building up of the Body of Christ—vv. 11-12.

   c. By the growth in the divine life, growing into the Head in all things—vv. 13, 15.

6. To be in the common fellowship of the enjoyment of Christ as the believers' common portion for the keeping of the oneness of the Body to witness that Christ is neither divisible nor divided—1 Cor. 1:2, 9-13.

7. To have the common fellowship in the spirit

and to have the common thinking and common love in one spirit, with one soul, and on one common standing for the testimony of the oneness of the Body of Christ—Phil. 2:1-2; 1:27.

8. To live and walk by the Spirit (Gal. 5:16, 25) and walk according to the mingled spirit (Rom. 8:4), setting our mind on the mingled spirit, being indwelt by the pneumatic Christ, the indwelling Spirit, to impart life within us and for us to put to death the practices of the body—Rom. 8:4, 6, 9-13.

9. To be conformed to the death of Christ, to have the self, natural man, flesh, distorted disposition, peculiarities, personal preference and tastes, etc., all crucified with Christ by the power of the resurrection of Christ—Phil. 3:10.

10. To magnify Christ through living Him by the bountiful supply of the Spirit of Jesus Christ—Phil. 1:19-21.

11. To minister Christ, dispensing Him, to all contacts.

12. To discern the spirit, which is of power, love, and sobermindedness, from the soul—Heb. 4:12; 2 Tim. 1:7.

B. The builders of the divine building:

1. Christ the Head, who speaks the words of God, imparts the divine life and gives the Spirit without measure—Matt. 16:18; John 3:34.

2. The gifted persons, especially the apostles and the prophets, perfect the saints for the building up of the Body of Christ—Eph. 4:11-12.

3. The perfected saints share the burden of the perfecting, gifted persons.

4. The entire Body—Eph. 4:16:
   a. Through every joint of the rich supply.
   b. Through the operation in the measure of each one part.
   c. By the growth of the Body unto the building up of itself in love.

5. Christ makes His home in the hearts of the saints through the strengthening with power through the Spirit into their inner man unto the fullness of the Triune God for His expression— Eph. 3:16-19.

6. The Triune God builds the abodes in the Father's house through the Spirit remaining within the lover of Christ, and the Father and the Son visit the lover of Christ to make the mutual abode—John 14:23.

C. The foundation of the divine building:

1. The redeeming and saving Christ—1 Cor. 3:11.

2. The apostles and the prophets with their revelation received of Christ as the rock and their teaching—Eph. 2:20; Matt. 16:18; Acts 2:42; 1 Tim. 1:4.

D. The materials of the divine building:

1. The Divine Trinity as the transformed precious items—gold, silver, and precious stones—1 Cor. 3:12:

a. Gold, signifying God the Father as the base of the divine building—Gen. 2:11; Rev. 21:18b, 21b.

b. Silver or bdellium and pearl, signifying Christ in His redeeming and life-releasing death and His life-dispensing resurrection— Gen. 2:12; Rev. 21:21a.

c. Precious stones, signifying the Spirit in His transforming and building work—Gen. 2:12; Rev. 21:19-20.

2. The transformed believers who are the divine plants transformed into the divine minerals— 1 Cor. 3:6-9.

3. Wood, in contrast to gold, signifies the nature of the natural man; grass, in contrast to silver, signifies the fallen man, the man of the flesh (1 Pet. 1:24); and stubble, in contrast to precious stones, signifies the work and living that issue from an earthen source: all these are not worthy

to be used as materials for the divine building—1 Cor. 3:12.

E. The work of the divine building:

   1. Renewing issues in transformation, and transformation issues in building up; the building
up of the jasper wall of the New Jerusalem
goes along with its transformation—Rev. 21:18a.

   2. It is the believers' growth in the divine life and
their being joined together in the divine life—
Eph. 4:15-16; 2:21.

   3. It is the believers' being built together in Christ
into a dwelling of God by the Spirit in their
spirit possessed by Christ, both of which are
mingled as one spirit—Eph. 2:22.

   4. It is also by the Spirit's operation, distributing
to each member different gifts for the building
up of the Body—1 Cor. 12:4, 7-11.

   5. The building work with gold, silver, and precious stones will be rewarded by Christ at His
coming back; if it is with wood, grass, and
stubble, it will be burned on the day of the
Lord's coming—1 Cor. 3:12-14.

F. The consummation of the divine building:

   1. The church in many localities as the house of
God to be God's dwelling place, the holy temple
in the Lord—1 Tim. 3:15; Eph. 2:21-22.

   2. The Body of Christ in the whole universe as
the expression of Christ—Eph. 1:23:

      a. In fact, all the believers in Christ have been
baptized into one Body by the Spirit—1 Cor.
12:13a.

      b. In practicality, based on the fact, all the
believers have to be built together into the
Body of Christ (Eph. 4:12) by the builders
of the divine building through the age of
the New Testament.

G. The destroyers of the divine building:

   1. Those who blow the wind of divisive teachings by stressing things other than the central

teaching concerning God's economy—Eph. 4:14; 1 Tim. 1:4.

2. Those who preach and teach heresies—2 Pet. 2:1; 2 John 7-11.

3. Those who are factious, sectarian—Titus 3:10.

4. Those who make divisions—Rom. 16:17.

5. Those who are ambitious for position—3 John 9.

6. Those who are wolves, not sparing the flock—Acts 20:29.

7. Those who speak perverted things to draw away the believers after them—Acts 20:30.

Prayer: O dear Lord, hear the singing of this hymn [*Hymns,* #840]. Lord, You know that we sing it from our heart. We sing it with a deep longing, according to Your desire, to be built up into one building. Lord, we thank You for Your speaking in the past and we look unto You for further speaking. Lord, cover us, defeat Your enemy, glorify Yourself, and bless all the dear saints. Amen.

In this message we come to the sixth section of God's organic salvation—the secret of building.

I. SOMETHING CRITICAL

The building is something which is critical to the accomplishment of God's eternal economy.

A. The Highest Requirement

To be built up with the fellow believers is the Lord's supreme and highest requirement to His faithful seekers according to one of the divine attributes of the Divine Trinity (John 17). Our oneness, to which we testify in the Lord's table meeting, is according to the divine oneness, which is an attribute of the Divine Trinity.

B. The Highest Virtue

Being built up with the fellow partakers of the divine life is the highest virtue of the one who pursues after Christ in God's eternal economy. Building is the highest requirement, and being built up is the highest virtue.

C. The Fallen Adamic Race
Not Able to Meet the Requirements

Not one of the descendants of the fallen adamic race has the capacity and ability to meet the high requirements of the kingdom of the heavens.

D. The Believers Being Qualified

Only the regenerated, sanctified, renewed, and transformed believers are qualified to fulfill the supreme requirements of the kingdom of the heavens.

E. The God-men Having the Divine Capacity

The God-men, who have the divine life, the divine nature, and the divine mind, and who participate in the divinity of God, have the divine capacity to carry out the divine requirements of the divine kingdom. God has qualified us by imparting His life into us, by sharing His nature with us, by making His mind our mind, and by transforming us with the element of His being. We praise Him for qualifying us and for giving us the divine capacity.

II. THE SECRET OF BUILDING

A. The Prerequisites

There are many prerequisites of the believers' building up in the church, the Body of Christ.

1. Realizing That the Lord Wants a Built Church

The first prerequisite is to realize that the Lord loves and wants to have, according to the desire of His heart, His good pleasure, a built church, not scattered individual believers. If we are scattered individuals, we can have no part in the building up of the church. It is crucial for us to see this.

2. Acknowledging That the Believers Have Been Baptized into One Body

Another prerequisite is that we acknowledge that all the believers have been baptized in one Spirit into one Body and that God has placed the members in the Body and blended all the Body together (1 Cor. 12:13a, 18, 24). If we see that God has already placed the members in the Body and has blended the Body together, we are built.

3. Being in Harmony and in One Accord

We also need to be in harmony with the fellow believers and to be in one accord with the Body in prayer, which issues in the establishment of the church (Matt. 18:19; Acts 1:14). We need not only to have the oneness but also to be in sweet harmony with other believers and to be in one accord with the Body in prayer. If we cannot pray in one accord with the saints, we are not one with them. Praying together is a test concerning whether or not we are in one accord with all the saints.

4. Practicing the Oneness of the Divine Trinity

The believers need to practice the oneness of the Divine Trinity in the Divine Trinity as the Divine Trinity does (John 17:21-23). We need to ask ourselves what kind of oneness we are practicing. Some claim to be practicing the oneness of the Body, but they are actually practicing a sectarian, factious oneness. The oneness of the Body is the oneness of the Triune God. We practice the oneness of the Divine Trinity not in ourselves but in the Divine Trinity. The three of the Divine Trinity—the Father, the Son, and the Spirit—are continually practicing the divine oneness. For example, the Lord Jesus said, "I and the Father are one" (John 10:30). The oneness of the Father and the Son includes the Spirit, who is the consummation and totality of the Triune God. The Spirit is also the Triune God reaching us. When Christ came into us, He came as the Spirit. Wherever the Father and the Son are, there the Spirit is also.

a. By the Divine Life

We practice the oneness of the Divine Trinity by the divine life with its source, the divine name of the Father (17:2-3, 6, 26). The name denotes the person—the Father, who is the source of life.

b. By the Divine Word

We practice the oneness of the Divine Trinity also by the divine word as the truth that sanctifies the believers from the world (vv. 14-19). We are separated from the world and are holy unto God.

c. By the Divine Glory

Furthermore, we practice the oneness of the Divine Trinity by the divine glory—the divine sonship with the Father's life and nature as the divine right to express the Father (vv. 22, 24). Sonship is composed of the divine life and the divine nature. Anyone who does not have the divine life and nature is not a son of God, for such a one does not have the divine sonship. The divine sonship implies God the Father's life and nature. This sonship is the right for us to express the Father. Actually, the only one who has this right is the Son of God. God the Father first gave His glory to His Son, and then His Son passed on this glory to us who, as sons of God, have God's life and nature as our sonship and as the right to express Him.

5. Keeping the Oneness of the Spirit

The next prerequisite is to keep the oneness of the Spirit diligently (Eph. 4:3). We keep this oneness in the constitution of the Body with the Divine Trinity (4:4-6) as the source (the Father), the element (the Son), and the essence (the Spirit). We also keep this oneness through the perfection by the gifted members for the building up of the Body of Christ (vv. 11-12). This means that keeping the oneness is related not only to the Triune God but also to the gifted persons—the apostles, the prophets, the evangelists, and the shepherds and teachers. Moreover, we keep the oneness by the growth in the divine life, growing into the Head in all things (vv. 13, 15).

6. Being in the Common Fellowship

The believers also need to be in the common fellowship of the enjoyment of Christ as the believers' common portion for the keeping of the oneness of the Body to witness that Christ is neither divisible nor divided (1 Cor. 1:2, 9-13).

7. Having the Common Fellowship, Thinking, and Love

Another prerequisite is that the believers have the common fellowship in the spirit and have the common thinking and common love in one spirit, with one soul, and on one common standing for the testimony of the oneness of the Body of Christ (Phil. 2:1-2; 1:27). If you have fellowship only in your district, that is not common fellowship but a particular fellowship. The common fellowship is universal. Our fellowship, therefore, must be universal.

8. *Living and Walking by the Spirit*

Next, the believers should live and walk by the Spirit (Gal. 5:16, 25) and walk according to the mingled spirit (Rom. 8:4), setting their mind on the mingled spirit, which is indwelt by the pneumatic Christ, the indwelling Spirit, to impart life within them and for them to put to death the practices of the body (Rom. 8:4, 6, 9-13).

9. *Being Conformed to the Death of Christ*

A further prerequisite for entering into the building is that we be conformed to the death of Christ, to have the self, natural man, flesh, distorted disposition, peculiarities, personal preference and tastes, etc., crucified with Christ by the power of the resurrection of Christ (Phil. 3:10).

10. *Magnifying Christ*

If we would enter into the building, we need to magnify Christ through living Him by the bountiful supply of the Spirit of Jesus Christ (Phil. 1:19-21).

11. *Ministering Christ*

A further prerequisite is that we minister Christ, dispensing Him, to all contacts.

12. *Discerning the Spirit from the Soul*

We need to discern the spirit, which is of power, love, and sobermindedness, from the soul (Heb. 4:12; 2 Tim. 1:7). All these twelve points are prerequisites for us to be built up together.

B. The Builders of the Divine Building

At this juncture we need to go on to consider the builders of the divine building. Some may think that Christ alone builds the church. However, the New Testament reveals that although Christ surely is building the church, He is not the only builder of the divine building.

1. Christ the Head

The first builder is Christ the Head, who speaks the words of God, imparts the divine life, and gives the Spirit without measure (Matt. 16:18; John 3:34). Unless we have enjoyed the impartation of the divine life and have received the Spirit without measure, we can have no part in the divine building, for the Lord Jesus cannot build us into the divine building. Yes, the Lord is building the church, but we must be those who are listening to His word, partaking of His divine life, and sharing His immeasurable Spirit, that is, sharing His Spirit immeasurably.

2. The Gifted Persons

The gifted persons, especially the apostles and the prophets, perfect the saints for the building up of the Body of Christ (Eph. 4:11-12).

3. The Perfected Saints

The perfected saints share the burden of the perfecting, gifted persons. Thus, the builders include Christ, the gifted persons, and the perfected saints.

4. The Entire Body

The entire Body also is a builder (Eph. 4:16). The entire Body builds through every joint of the rich supply, through the operation in the measure of each one part, and by the growth of the Body unto the building up of itself in love. How then can anyone claim that Christ is the only builder? Unless the entire Body builds, the Body cannot be built up. The whole Body has to build the Body itself in love.

5. Christ Making His Home in the Saints' Hearts

Christ makes His home in the hearts of the saints through the strengthening with power through the Spirit into their inner man unto the fullness of the Triune God for His expression (Eph. 3:16-19). Christ not only builds up the Body; He also seeks to make His home in the hearts of the believers. Is Christ now making His home in your heart? If He is to make His home in your heart, you need to be strengthened by God the Father with power and through His Spirit into your inner man. Then Christ will build up His home in your heart "unto all the fullness of God" (v. 19). Christ's making His home in our heart results in our being filled unto all the fullness of God for His universal expression.

6. The Triune God Building the Abodes

The Triune God builds the abodes in the Father's house through the Spirit remaining within the lover of Christ, and the Father and the Son visit the lover of Christ to make the mutual abode (John 14:23). In the Father's house there are many abodes, which are built by the Triune God through the Spirit. This abode is a mutual dwelling place for the believer and the Triune God.

C. The Foundation of the Divine Building

1. The Redeeming and Saving Christ

The foundation of the divine building is the redeeming and saving Christ (1 Cor. 3:11). He is the unique foundation, and, as Paul says, "another foundation no one is able to lay."

2. The Revelation Given to the Apostles and Prophets

The foundation is also the apostles and the prophets with their revelation received of Christ as the rock and their teaching (Eph. 2:20; Matt. 16:18; Acts 2:42; 1 Tim. 1:4). In Matthew 16:16 Peter declared, "You are the Christ, the Son of the living God." The Lord Jesus told Peter that he was blessed to have received such a revelation, and then, referring to this revelation, He went on to say, "Upon this rock I will build My church" (v. 18). From this we see that the foundation is not only Christ Himself but also the "rock" of the revelation received by the apostles and prophets and the apostles' teaching, which actually includes the entire New Testament. Therefore, the foundation for the building is both Christ and the revelation given to the apostles and prophets. This is the foundation upon which we are building today.

D. The Materials of the Divine Building

1. The Divine Trinity as the Precious Items

First, the materials of the divine building are the Divine Trinity as the transformed precious items—gold, silver, and precious stones (1 Cor. 3:12). Paul warns us to take heed, to be careful about, how we build upon Christ as the foundation. We must use the right materials, which are gold, silver, and precious stones. Gold signifies God the Father as the base of the divine building (Gen. 2:11; Rev. 21:18, 21). Silver or bdellium and pearl signify Christ in His redeeming and life-releasing death and His life-dispensing resurrection (Gen. 2:12; Rev. 21:21). Precious stones signify the Spirit in His transforming and building up work (Gen. 2:12; Rev. 21:19-20).

2. The Transformed Believers

The materials also include the transformed believers who are the divine plants transformed into the divine minerals (1 Cor. 3:6-9).

3. The Unworthy Materials

Wood, in contrast to gold, signifies the nature of the natural man; grass, in contrast to silver, signifies the fallen man, the man of the flesh (1 Pet. 1:24); and stubble, in contrast to precious stones, signifies the work and living that issue from an earthen source. All these are not worthy to be used as materials for the divine building (1 Cor. 3:12).

The natural man cannot be used for the divine building. The natural man, the man created by God, may be good but is not regenerated and transformed, and thus is not the proper material for the building. The fallen man, the man of the flesh, has no part in the building. Furthermore, the work and living that issue from an earthen source are not worthy of the divine building. These materials should not be used in the divine building. You should build only with the precious materials, that is, with the Triune God and with the transformed believers. If we see this, we will realize that in the building up of the church, we must put ourselves aside, including whatever we are as a naturally good man or as a fallen, fleshly man. Everything that issues from an earthen source must also be put aside. Natural things and worldly things cannot be adopted for the building up of the church, the Body of Christ.

E. The Work of the Divine Building

1. Renewing, Transformation, and Building Up

The work of the divine building is carried out through renewing and transformation. Renewing issues in transformation, and transformation issues in building up. The building up of the jasper wall of the New Jerusalem goes along with its transformation (Rev. 21:18a). We need to be renewed and transformed, and then we can do the work of building.

2. The Believers' Growth in the Divine Life

The work of the divine building is the believers' growth in the divine life and their being joined together in the divine life (Eph. 4:15-16; 2:21). We need to grow up together and be joined together in the divine life. This growing and joining together is the building. The actual building is our growth and our union in the divine life. When we grow in the divine life and when we are joined together in the divine life, we are in the building.

3. The Believers' Being Built Together in Christ

The work of the divine building is also the believers' being built together in Christ into a dwelling of God by the Spirit in their spirit possessed by Christ, both of which are mingled as one spirit (Eph. 2:22). If we are experiencing this, we are doing the work of building up the Body.

4. The Spirit's Operation

The building is also by the Spirit's operation, distributing to each member different gifts for the building up of the Body (1 Cor. 12:4, 7-11). The Spirit's distributing different gifts to different members is the actual building work.

5. Rewarded by Christ

The building work with gold, silver, and precious stones will be rewarded by Christ at His coming back. However, if the work is with wood, grass, and stubble, it will be burned on the day of the Lord's coming (1 Cor. 3:12-14). If your work in building up the church is by your natural man, by your fallen, fleshly man, or by anything that issues from an earthen source, your work will not be rewarded but instead it will be burned.

The New Testament reveals that at the end of this age there will be three burnings. Revelation 17:16 indicates that Catholicism will be burned. In Matthew 13 the Lord Jesus indicates that the tares, the false Christians in Christianity, will be burned (vv. 24-30, 40-41). The false Christians have caused great damage to God's economy. When the Lord Jesus comes back, He will send His angels to collect all the tares, bind them into bundles, and burn them. This is the burning of the false believers in Protestantism. The third burning will be that mentioned in 1 Corinthians 3:13-15: "The work of each will become manifest; for the day will declare it, because it is revealed by fire, and the fire itself will prove each one's work, of what sort it is. If anyone's work which he has built upon the foundation remains, he will receive a reward; if anyone's work is consumed, he will suffer loss, but he himself will be saved, yet so as through fire." If we build the church with God the Father as gold, with God the Son as silver, and with God the Spirit as precious stones, we will receive the reward. However, if we do the work of the building by the natural man, by the fallen man, and with things that issue from the earthen source, our work will be burned, yet we ourselves will be saved. We all need to consider how we are building the church. We should be those who are building with the Divine Trinity as the precious and transformed materials.

F. The Consummation of the Divine Building

1. The Church as the House of God

The consummation, the accomplishment, of the divine building is the church in many localities as the house of God to be God's dwelling place, the holy temple in the Lord (1 Tim. 3:15; Eph. 2:21-22).

2. The Body of Christ

The consummation is also the Body of Christ in the whole universe as the expression of Christ (Eph. 1:23). All the churches are one Body, and the co-workers should be doing not a regional work but a universal work for the universal Body. In fact, all the believers in Christ have been baptized into one Body by the Spirit (1 Cor. 12:13a). In practicality, based on the fact, all the believers have to be built together into the Body of Christ (Eph. 4:12) by the builders of the divine building through the age of the New Testament.

G. The Destroyers of the Divine Building

In addition to all the positive things which we have covered in this message, there is one category of negative persons—the destroyers of the divine building. According to the New Testament there are seven kinds of destroyers:

1. Those who blow the wind of divisive teachings by stressing things other than the central teaching concerning God's economy (Eph. 4:14; 1 Tim. 1:4).

2. Those who preach and teach heresies (2 Pet. 2:1; 2 John 7-11).

3. Those who are factious, sectarian (Titus 3:10).

4. Those who make divisions (Rom. 16:17).

5. Those who are ambitious for position (3 John 9).

6. Those who are wolves, not sparing the flock (Acts 20:29).

7. Those who speak perverted things to draw away the believers after them (Acts 20:30).

When some hear that there are destroyers of the divine building, they may say, "Is this not the divine building, the building of God? How can anyone destroy it?" In a sense, no one can destroy the divine building. Nevertheless, many are stirred up by the enemy and try their best to destroy the building of the church. As we have indicated, the first kind of destroyers are those who blow the wind of divisive teachings by stressing things other than the central teaching concerning God's economy. For example, the New Testament teaching regarding baptism by immersion is a minor teaching, but the Southern Baptists make it a major teaching and in so doing their teaching becomes divisive. The principle is the same with every denomination: they are built upon a particular teaching, and they teach things other than the central teaching concerning God's economy. Regarding such a situation, Paul exhorted Timothy to remain in Ephesus in order that he might "charge certain ones not to teach different things... rather than God's economy, which is in faith" (1 Tim. 1:3-4). We all need to be careful not to take any teaching, even a scriptural one, and make it a central teaching. Throughout the years Brother Nee and I have not stressed anything other than the central line of God's economy concerning the church for the producing of the Body to consummate the New Jerusalem. This central teaching is not divisive; on the contrary, it builds up the Body.

CHAPTER FIVE

THE SECRET OF CONFORMATION
AND GLORIFICATION

OUTLINE

I. The secret of conformation—the seventh section of God's organic salvation:

   A. God's intention is to make man like Him in His divine life, nature, and image as His expression, but not in His Godhead.

   B. God regenerates the believers in Christ with His divine life that they may begin to participate in His divinity.

   C. After being regenerated, the regenerated believers begin to grow through:

      1. The divine feeding,

      2. The divine sanctification,

      3. The divine renewing,

      4. The divine transformation in the divine life,

   D. Until they mature in the divine life by the maturing Spirit in the believers' spirit enriched with Christ to be a full-grown man, at the measure of the stature of the fullness of Christ—Col. 1:28; Eph. 4:13,

   E. Conformed to the image of Christ the firstborn Son of God—Rom. 8:29,

   F. Who was begotten by God in His resurrection with both His divinity and His enlivened and uplifted humanity, possessing two natures, both divine and human—Acts 13:33; Rom. 1:4; 1 Pet. 3:18.

   G. Thus, the conformation of the believers is the consummation of their transformation in the divine life through which they participate in God's divinity in full.

II. The secret of glorification—the eighth section of God's organic salvation:

A. In regeneration God seals the regenerated believers with His Spirit—Eph. 1:13.

B. This sealing of the sealing Spirit is like inking, saturating the sealed believers from within with the glorious life element of God throughout their life, resulting in the redemption of their body—Eph. 4:30; Rom. 8:23.

C. At the time of the rapture of the believers who are matured in the divine life, they will be brought in their spirit exulting with Christ from without into the glory of God for their glorification—Rom. 8:30; Heb. 2:10.

D. Thus, the matured believers will be glorified from within through the lifelong saturation with the glory of God and from without through their being brought into God's glory.

E. The glorification of the matured believers is their top portion of their divine sonship in God's organic salvation—which they received at the time of their regeneration—Gal. 4:5; Rom. 8:23.

F. The redemption of the believers' body is the transfiguration of their body at the Lord's coming back—Phil. 3:20-21.

G. The word *redemption* indicates it is judicial because the believers' redeemed body is of the fallen old creation—this redemption of the believers' body is the finalization of God's judicial redemption; the word *transfiguration* indicates it is organic because the transfiguration of the believers' body is by the divine life within them.

H. The divine glorification of the glorified believers makes the consummated believers participate in God's divinity to the uttermost.

Prayer: Lord, we extol You again, acknowledging that You are the One whom God sent to speak His words and that You are also the One who gives the Spirit, the bountiful Spirit, all-inclusive Spirit, life-giving Spirit, the indwelling Spirit, not by measure. Hallelujah! Oh, this really meets our need! We need the word and we need the Spirit. We need the words of life and we need the Spirit of life. Lord, we thank You that through the years You have been speaking Your word to Your recovery and that You have been also giving Your Spirit to Your recovery. Thank You for Your revelation and for Your move. We praise You that You have shown us Your economy, with Christ as the centrality and the universality. Oh, what a Christ we have! We thank You for Your organic salvation, we thank You for Your Christ, and we thank You for the Spirit. Lord, we are still here receiving Your revelation with Your vision. Every day You give us new words. We thank You for showing us that we participate in God's divinity. We have received Your life and Your nature, and by these we participate in God's divinity. We thank You that we also have the divine mind, the mind of Christ, and by this also we participate in God's divinity. We thank You that we are enjoying the riches of Christ as the element that transforms us metabolically so that by this metabolism we can participate in God's divinity to the fullest. Lord, we are here before You to enjoy something further. Lord, as we come to the matters of conformation and glorification, we ask You to be with us and to give us the words, the new language for a new culture. Once again, we pray that You will cover us from Your enemy, the troublemaker. Bind him and put him into the corner. Amen.

I. THE SECRET OF CONFORMATION

Conformation is the seventh section of God's organic salvation.

A. God's Intention

God's intention is to make man like Him in His divine life, in His divine nature, and in His image as His expression, but not in His Godhead. For God to make man like Him in this way actually means to make man God. God has imparted Himself into us to make us the same as He is in life and in nature but not in His Godhead. This is the divine intention.

B. God Regenerating the Believers

In order to carry out His intention, God regenerates the believers in Christ with His divine life that they may begin to participate in His divinity. Since we, the believers in Christ, participate in God's divinity, we are gods. Second Peter 1:4 says that we partake of the divine nature. To partake of something is to participate in that thing. We partake of God's nature and thus we participate in God's divinity. The divine One has imparted Himself into us to become our being. He dispenses Himself into us to be our life, our nature, our mind, and everything to us. If we are not those who participate in God's divinity, then who participates in it? The angels cannot participate in God's divinity, because they do not possess anything of God as we do. We are more blessed than the angels, for they are merely God's servants, but we are God's sons, possessing God's divinity.

C. The Believers Beginning to Grow

After they have been regenerated, the regenerated believers begin to grow.

1. Feeding

Just as a child grows through feeding, the regenerated believers grow through the divine feeding. However, many of today's Christians are not growing, because with them there is no feeding. Due to their lack of feeding, they also lack the proper sanctification, renewing, and transformation.

2. Sanctification

We grow first through the divine feeding and then through the divine sanctification. Sanctification causes us to grow. The more we are sanctified, the more we grow. In John 17:17-19 the Lord Jesus prayed, saying, "Sanctify them in the truth; Your word is truth. As You have sent Me into the world, I also have sent them into the world. And for their sake

I sanctify Myself, that they themselves also may be sanctified in truth." To be sanctified is to be separated from the world. Daily we need to be sanctified, separated from the world, so that through this sanctification we may grow.

3. Renewing

The regenerated believers grow also through the divine renewing. Renewing is therefore a factor of growth in the divine life.

4. Transformation

The divine transformation in the divine life is a strong factor of the believers' growth. Without the divine transformation we cannot grow. Many of today's Christians do not grow because they do not have the divine feeding, the divine sanctification, the divine renewing, and the divine transformation.

D. Maturing in the Divine Life

The believers need to grow until they mature in the divine life by the maturing Spirit in their spirit enriched with Christ to be a full-grown man, at the measure of the stature of the fullness of Christ (Col. 1:28; Eph. 4:13). We cannot mature without the proper supply, and this supply is the life-giving Spirit, who is the maturing Spirit in the believers' spirit enriched with Christ. We can testify that our spirit is enriched with Christ. Eventually, we will be a full-grown man, at the measure of the stature of the fullness of Christ. In Ephesians 4:13 the word *fullness* refers to the Body of Christ. We have to be fully matured in order to be a fully grown man at the measure of the stature of the Body of Christ.

E. Conformed to the Image of Christ

In God's organic salvation the believers will be conformed to the image of Christ the firstborn Son of God (Rom. 8:29).

F. The Firstborn Son of God Begotten by God in His Resurrection

As the firstborn Son of God, Christ was begotten by God in His resurrection with both His divinity and His enlivened and uplifted humanity, possessing two natures, both divine and human (Acts 13:33; Rom. 1:4; 1 Pet. 3:18).

In resurrection Christ's humanity was sanctified, enlivened, uplifted, and transformed. Our humanity had become fallen and has been redeemed by Christ. His humanity did not need to be redeemed, but His humanity, which died on the cross, needed to be sanctified, enlivened, uplifted, and transformed. Through resurrection the Lord's dead humanity was sanctified, enlivened, uplifted, and transformed into the divine sonship. In resurrection He was begotten of God to be the firstborn Son of God both with His divinity and with His sanctified, enlivened, uplifted, and transformed humanity. The firstborn Son of God was therefore begotten of God with both divinity and humanity, and we are being conformed to His image.

G. The Consummation of Transformation

The conformation of the believers is the consummation of their transformation in the divine life through which they participate in God's divinity in full.

II. THE SECRET OF GLORIFICATION

Glorification is the eighth section of God's organic salvation.

A. The Believers Sealed with God's Spirit

In regeneration God seals the regenerated believers with His Spirit (Eph. 1:13). When a piece of paper is sealed with ink, the ink saturates the paper. This is an illustration of the fact that the sealing of the Spirit involves the believers' being saturated with the Spirit.

B. The Sealing Spirit Saturating the Believers

The sealing of the sealing Spirit is like inking, saturating the sealed believers from within with the glorious life element of God throughout their life, resulting in the redemption of their body (Eph. 4:30; Rom. 8:23). Throughout our entire Christian life, this sealing, this "inking," is saturating our being from within. With what does the sealing Spirit seal the believers? The Spirit is sealing them with the glory of the divine life. The glory of the divine life is the "ink," and throughout the believers' life this ink by the "inking" is saturating their entire being from within with the glorious life element of God.

Such a saturating will eventually result in the redemption of our body. Ephesians 4:30 tells us that we are sealed by the Holy Spirit "unto the day of redemption." Here the word *unto* means "resulting in" or "for." This sealing is for the redemption of our body and it will result in the redemption of our body. From the time we were saved and regenerated, the Spirit as the seal in us has been sealing us continually with the glorious life element of God unto the day of the redemption of our body.

C. The Believers Brought into the Glory of God

At the time of the rapture of the believers who are matured in the divine life, they will be brought in their spirit exulting with Christ from without into the glory of God for their glorification (Rom. 8:30; Heb. 2:10).

D. The Matured Believers Being Glorified

The matured believers will be glorified from within through the lifelong saturation with the glory of God and from without through their being brought into God's glory.

At present the "inking" is saturating us with God's glory from within. This is a lifelong matter. Eventually, we will be brought into God's glory in an outward way. Whereas the inner saturating is a lifelong process, our being brought into God's glory outwardly will be instantaneous. In an instant, in the twinkling of an eye, we will be brought into God's glory. Thus, the matured believers will be glorified from within through the lifelong saturation with the glory of God and from without through their being brought into God's glory.

E. The Top Portion of the Divine Sonship

The glorification of the matured believers is the top portion of their divine sonship in God's organic salvation, which sonship they received at the time of their regeneration (Gal. 4:5; Rom. 8:23). In God's organic salvation the matter of sonship is very critical and central. The redemption of our body is the highest enjoyment of the sonship. Romans 8:23 says, "We ourselves groan in ourselves, eagerly awaiting sonship, the redemption of our body." As an elderly person with a number of physical infirmities, I often groan because of the weakness of my body. However, while I am groaning I am awaiting sonship, the redemption of my body. The day is coming when our body will be redeemed and we will enter into the full enjoyment of the divine sonship.

F. The Redemption and Transfiguration of the Body

The redemption of the believers' body is the transfiguration of their body at the Lord's coming back (Phil. 3:20-21).

G. The Redemption of the Body Being Judicial and the Transfiguration of the Body Being Organic

The word *redemption* indicates that the redemption of the body is judicial because the believers' redeemed body is of the fallen old creation. This redemption of the believers' body is the finalization of God's judicial redemption. The word *transfiguration* indicates that the redemption of the believers' body is organic because the transfiguration of their body is by the divine life within them.

H. Participating in God's Divinity to the Uttermost

The divine glorification of the glorified believers makes the consummated believers participate in God's divinity to the uttermost.

In these messages we have considered the eight sections of God's organic salvation: regeneration, feeding, sanctification, renewing, transformation, building, conformation, and glorification. God's goal in these eight sections of His organic salvation is simply to make us God, that is, to make us a duplication, a xerox copy, of God.

Through regeneration God imparted His life into our being. Now we have the divine life, and we are also partaking of the divine nature. In addition, we have God's mind and the element of Christ's unsearchable riches. To have the riches of Christ means that we have God's being. Therefore, we have God's life, God's nature, God's mind, and God's being. Eventually, we will be conformed to the image of Christ, the first God-man, and we will be fully saturated with the glory of the divine life and be brought into God's glory. At that time we will have God's life, God's nature, God's mind, God's being, and God's glory and we will bear God's image. We will surely have become God in life, in nature, and in expression but not in the Godhead. If such a person is not God, what is he? When our body is redeemed and transfigured and we thereby enjoy the highest portion of the divine sonship, we will be able to say, "Hallelujah! I have been made God. Praise the Lord that I have God's life, God's nature, God's mind, God's being, and God's glory and that I am in God's image!"

CHAPTER SIX

THE SECRET OF THE INTENSIFIED WORK
OF GOD'S ORGANIC SALVATION

OUTLINE

I. The three sections of Christ's ministry:

    A. The first section of His earthly ministry, accomplished by Him judicially in the flesh from His incarnation to His death.

    B. The second section of His heavenly ministry, carried out by Him as the life-giving Spirit, organically in the mystical realm, from His resurrection to the end of the millennium.

    C. The third section of His sevenfold intensified heavenly ministry, carried out by Him as the sevenfold intensified life-giving Spirit, sevenfold intensified organically in the mystical realm, from the degradation of the church to the full consummation of the New Jerusalem.

II. The secret of the intensified work of God's organic salvation:

    A. The degradation of the church:

        1. At the end of the apostle Paul's ministry, around the A.D. 60s:

            a. All the believers in Asia turned away from him—2 Tim. 1:15.

            b. Hymenaeus and Philetus said that the resurrection had already taken place—2:17-18.

            c. The co-worker of the apostle, Demas, loved the present age and abandoned him—4:10.

            d. Alexander the coppersmith did many evil things to the apostle and greatly opposed the apostle's words—vv. 14-15.

       e. At the apostle's first defense no one was with him to support him, but all abandoned him—v. 16.

  2. At the end of the apostle Peter's ministry, around the A.D. 60s:

       a. False teachers were teaching heresy, denying the Lord's redemption—2 Pet. 2:1.

       b. The evil ones forsook the straight way, going astray and following the way of Balaam, who loved the wages of unrighteousness—v. 15.

       c. Mockers were mocking, not believing in the Lord's coming back—3:3-4.

       d. The unlearned and unstable ones twisted the teachings of the apostle Paul—vv. 15-16.

  3. At the end of the apostle John's ministry, around the A.D. 90s:

       a. Many antichrists lied, denying that Jesus is the Christ—1 John 2:18, 22.

       b. Many false prophets, by the spirit of deception, did not confess that Christ came in the flesh—4:1-2, 6.

       c. Many deceivers as antichrists, not confessing that Christ came in the flesh, taught beyond the teaching of Christ—2 John 7, 9-11.

       d. Diotrephes, loving to be first in the church, did not receive the apostles, babbling evil words against them, and forbade those intending to receive the brothers and cast them out of the church—3 John 9-10.

B. The intensification of Christ:

  1. Christ as the life-giving Spirit was intensified to be the seven Spirits, the sevenfold intensified life-giving Spirit—Rev. 1:4; 4:5; 5:6:

       a. The sevenfold intensified Spirit became the second, the center, of the Divine Trinity—1:4.

       b. The sevenfold intensified Spirit, as the seven Spirits, is the seven lamps burning before the throne of God—4:5.

    c. The sevenfold intensified Spirit, as the seven Spirits, is the seven eyes of the Lamb sent forth into all the earth, searching and infusing all the churches and all the saints with His eyes—5:6.

2. To save the believers from:

    a. The formal church life and the loss of the first love to the Lord, the shining capacity of the lampstand, and the enjoyment of Christ as life in the church in Ephesus—2:1-7.

    b. The defeat that leads to the taste of the second death in the church in Smyrna—vv. 8-11.

    c. The worldliness in union with the world as a marriage and the teaching of Balaam and the Nicolaitans in the church in Pergamos—vv. 12-17.

    d. Fornication, idolatry, demonic teaching, and satanic depths in Catholicism, signified by the church in Thyatira—vv. 18-29.

    e. The spiritual death—dead and dying—in Protestantism, signified by the church in Sardis—3:1-6.

    f. The losing of the crown, which has been gained already in Brethrenism, signified by the church in Philadelphia—vv. 7-13.

    g. The lukewarmness and the Christlessness in degraded Brethrenism, signified by the church in Laodicea—vv. 14-22.

3. By:

    a. The speaking of the unlimited life-releasing sevenfold intensified pneumatic Christ to the seven churches at the beginning of each epistle respectively becoming the speaking of the sevenfold intensified, all-inclusive, life-giving Spirit to all the seven churches at the end of each epistle universally—2:1, 7, 8, 11, 12, 17, 18, 29; 3:1, 6, 7, 13, 14, 22.

        b. The participation of the overcoming saints
           who are living in their spirit drawn by the
           Lamb—1:10; 4:2; 17:3; 21:10; 14:4.

   4. For:

        a. Producing the overcomers to build up the
           Body of Christ for the initial consummation
           of the New Jerusalem in the kingdom age
           (2:7) and the full consummation of the
           New Jerusalem in the new heaven and new
           earth— 21:2.

        b. The complete preparation of the bride of
           Christ the Bridegroom, to have His trium-
           phant wedding in the millennium for His
           satisfaction according to His good pleasure—
           19:7-9.

        c. The formation of the bridal army for Christ
           to defeat and destroy His top enemies
           in humanity, the Antichrist and his false
           prophet—vv. 11-21; 17:14.

        d. The binding of Satan and the casting of
           him into the abyss for one thousand years—
           20:1-3.

        e. The bringing in of the kingdom of Christ
           and of God which will be the millennium—
           vv. 4-6.

   5. The final outcome:

        a. The ultimately consummated Spirit as the
           consummation of the processed Triune God
           becomes the Bridegroom,

        b. And the aggregate of the overcoming saints
           becomes the bride of the universal romance,

        c. Between the redeeming God and His re-
           deemed man,

        d. As the conclusion of the entire Scriptures—
           22:17.

III. An appendix:

The words, listed as follows, concerning the compounded, all-inclusive, life-giving, and indwelling Spirit,
unveil also the secret of God's organic salvation:

A. The consummated Spirit as the second Paraclete (the Comforter), the realization of Christ as the first Paraclete, takes care of the believers, especially in the matter of the Divine Trinity being the main, life element of the organic salvation of God—John 14:16-18.

B. The indwelling Spirit joins in to help the believers in their weakness and He Himself intercedes by groaning in the spirit of the believers that all things may work together for good to those who love God that they may be conformed to the image of His Son that He might be the Firstborn among many brothers—Rom. 8:26, 28-29.

C. The believer who is joined to the Lord can experience the Lord to the climax, even to be one spirit with the Lord (God)—1 Cor. 6:17.

D. The Father strengthens the believers, according to the riches of His glory, with power through His Spirit into the believers' inner man, for Christ to make His home in the believers' heart that they may be filled unto the fullness of the Triune God for His corporate expression—Eph. 3:16-19.

E. The apostle who sought to know Christ and gain Him was enabled to do all things in Christ who empowered him by His Spirit of bountiful supply—Phil. 3:10a, 12; 4:13; 1:19.

Prayer: Lord, we extol You again. Essentially You are the second One of the Trinity, yet economically You first became flesh, then You became the life-giving Spirit, and now You are the intensified sevenfold Spirit. We thank You that, essentially, You have never changed. From eternity to eternity You remain the same. We thank You also that, economically, You have changed. You changed by becoming flesh. Then as the last Adam in the flesh You changed again by becoming the life-giving Spirit. As the life-giving Spirit You changed again, and now You are the sevenfold intensified Spirit. We praise You for what You did to accomplish God's judicial redemption. We praise You for what You are doing to accomplish God's salvation organically and for what You are doing in Your intensification to carry out God's economy. How we worship You! Lord, we ask You to teach us concerning all these things. We believe that this is Your complete and perfect theology. Lord, save Your people so that they may be transformed and become the precious materials—gold, silver, and precious stones—and not remain in a situation of wood, grass, and stubble. Lord, we fear and tremble, fearing that we might be in the second category. Lord, we want to be in the first category, having all the precious, transformed materials. We pray that You will cover us. Lord, You are the Alpha and Omega. You have given us a good beginning, and now we ask You to give us a good conclusion. Amen.

The secret of the intensified work of God's organic salvation is something in addition to God's organic salvation. As we have seen, God's organic salvation is of eight sections, from regeneration through glorification. However, in order for God's economy to be completed and consummated, that is, for God to have the New Jerusalem, something further is needed. After His resurrection and in His heavenly ministry, the Lord Jesus established many churches, but not long afterward the churches became degraded. This made it necessary for Christ, who had become the life-giving Spirit in resurrection, to intensify Himself to be the sevenfold intensified Spirit. This is clearly revealed in the book of Revelation (1:4; 3:1; 4:5; 5:6).

I. THE THREE SECTIONS
OF CHRIST'S MINISTRY

Christians often say that Christ's ministry is of two parts or sections—His earthly ministry and His heavenly ministry. However, Christ's ministry is actually of three sections. The third section of His ministry is the sevenfold intensified heavenly ministry. This ministry is still His heavenly ministry, but it is a heavenly ministry that has been intensified sevenfold.

A. The First Section

The first section of Christ's ministry was His earthly ministry. This ministry was accomplished by Him judicially in the flesh from His incarnation to His death. In His flesh He died for us according to the righteous requirements of God's law.

B. The Second Section

The second section of Christ's ministry is His heavenly ministry. This ministry is carried out by Him as the life-giving Spirit, organically in the mystical realm, from His resurrection to the end of the millennium. Christ's ministry in this section is altogether organic, for it is carried out by Him in His resurrection life.

C. The Third Section

The third section of Christ's ministry is His sevenfold intensified heavenly ministry. This ministry is carried out by Him as the sevenfold intensified life-giving Spirit, sevenfold intensified organically in the mystical realm, from the degradation of the church to the full consummation of the New Jerusalem. Now Christ is not only the life-giving Spirit—He is the sevenfold intensified life-giving Spirit carrying out His sevenfold intensified heavenly ministry. The first section of Christ's ministry was judicial, the second section is organic, and the third section is sevenfold intensified.

Very few Christians realize that today we should not be merely in Christ's heavenly ministry but in His sevenfold intensified heavenly ministry. We all need to be in the third section of Christ's ministry. Today the Lord is working not only as the life-giving Spirit but also as the sevenfold intensified Spirit. This Spirit may be compared to the shining of the sun spoken of in Isaiah 30:26, which says that in the millennium "the light of the sun shall be sevenfold." Today the Spirit who is filling us and saturating us is the sevenfold intensified life-giving Spirit. We all need to see this and then pray, "Lord, I worship You that You are working in me as the sevenfold intensified Spirit."

In the past some have tried to argue with us, saying that Christ cannot change and quoting Hebrews 13:8, which says, "Jesus Christ is the same yesterday and today, yes, even forever." Regarding this we would point out that Christ has not changed essentially, but He has changed economically. Essentially He is the same from eternity to eternity, but economically He has changed in three ways—by becoming flesh in His incarnation, by becoming the life-giving Spirit in His resurrection, and by intensifying Himself to be the sevenfold intensified life-giving Spirit in His intensification.

II. THE SECRET OF THE INTENSIFIED WORK OF GOD'S ORGANIC SALVATION

A. The Degradation of the Church

In considering the secret of the intensified work of God's organic salvation, the first matter we need to pay attention to is the degradation of the church. If there had been no degradation, there would have been no need for Christ to be intensified sevenfold. Christ's sevenfold intensification is due to the degradation of the church.

1. At the End of Paul's Ministry

The degradation of the church took place at the end of the apostle Paul's ministry, around the A.D. 60s.

a. The Believers Turning Away

All the believers in Asia turned away from Paul (2 Tim. 1:15). They turned away not from Paul's person but from his ministry.

b. Hymenaeus and Philetus

Hymenaeus and Philetus said that the resurrection had already taken place (2:17-18). They taught the heresy that there would be no resurrection.

c. Demas

Demas, a co-worker of the apostle Paul, loved the present age and abandoned Paul (4:10). This also was an aspect of the degradation of the church.

d. Alexander the Coppersmith

Alexander the coppersmith, who might have been quite close to Paul, did many evil things to the apostle and greatly opposed the apostle's words (vv. 14-15).

e. No One Being with Him

At the apostle's first defense no one was with him to support him, but all abandoned him (v. 16).

2. At the End of Peter's Ministry

The degradation at the end of the apostle Peter's ministry also took place around the A.D. 60s.

a. False Teachers

False teachers were teaching heresy, denying the Lord's redemption (2 Pet. 2:1).

b. Forsaking the Straight Way

The evil ones forsook the straight way, that is, the New Testament way, going astray and following the way of Balaam, who loved the wages of unrighteousness (v. 15).

c. Mockers

Mockers were mocking, not believing in the Lord's coming back (3:3-4).

d. Twisting Paul's Teachings

The unlearned and unstable ones twisted the teachings of the apostle Paul (vv. 15-16).

3. At the End of John's Ministry

The degradation at the end of the apostle John's ministry took place around the A.D. 90s.

a. Many Antichrists

Many antichrists lied, denying that Jesus is the Christ, the One anointed by God (1 John 2:18, 22).

b. Many False Prophets

Many false prophets, by the spirit of deception, did not confess that Christ came in the flesh (4:1-2, 6).

c. Many Deceivers

Many deceivers as antichrists, not confessing that Christ came in the flesh, taught beyond the teaching of Christ (2 John 7, 9-11).

d. Diotrephes

Diotrephes, who loved to be first in the church, did not receive the apostles, babbling evil words against them, and forbade those intending to receive the brothers and cast them out of the church (3 John 9-10).

From all the foregoing we can see what kind of degradation had come in. At the end of the ministry of the three main writers of the New Testament—Paul, Peter, and John—there was degradation. Because of this degradation, the life-giving Spirit, that is, the pneumatic Christ, had to be intensified sevenfold.

B. The Intensification of Christ

1. Intensified to Be the Seven Spirits

Christ as the life-giving Spirit was intensified to be the seven Spirits, the sevenfold intensified life-giving Spirit (Rev. 1:4; 4:5; 5:6).

a. The Center of the Divine Trinity

In Revelation 1:4 and 5 the Spirit becomes the second, the center, of the Divine Trinity. The sequence of the Divine Trinity in Matthew 28:19 is the Father, the Son, and the Spirit. There the Father as the source is the first, the Spirit is the last, and the Son is the center, the second. In Revelation 1:4 and 5 the sequence is changed: "Grace to you and peace from Him who is and who was and who is coming [the Father], and from the seven Spirits who are before His throne, and from Jesus Christ, the faithful Witness, the Firstborn of the dead, and the Ruler of the kings of the earth." This change of sequence reveals the importance of the function of the sevenfold intensified Spirit. There is a sense, however, in which the sequence actually has not changed, for as the Spirit, who is the consummation of the Triune God, Christ remains the center of the Divine Trinity.

b. The Seven Lamps

The sevenfold intensified Spirit, as the seven Spirits, is the seven lamps burning before the throne of God (4:5). Because of the degradation, many things should be burned. However, the lamps are mainly not for burning but for enlightening. When the lamps enlighten, they also burn.

c. The Seven Eyes of the Lamb

The sevenfold intensified Spirit, as the seven Spirits, is the seven eyes of the Lamb sent forth into all the earth, searching and infusing all the churches and all the saints with His eyes (5:6).

As the seven eyes of the Lamb, the seven Spirits are one with the Lamb. Your eyes are not separate from you yourself. When you look at someone, your eyes look at that one, and when your eyes look at someone, you yourself look at that one. The fact that the seven Spirits are the seven eyes of Christ the Lamb indicates that Christ and the Spirit are one. It is heretical to say the Spirit is not one with Christ. Just as the eyes of a person are not separate from the person, so the seven Spirits as the seven eyes of Christ are not separate from Christ. The seven Spirits are Christ Himself because they are the eyes of Christ. The seven Spirits are just Christ Himself pneumatically.

The seven Spirits as the seven eyes are for both searching and infusing. While your eyes are searching a person, they are infusing something of yourself into that person. With the seven Spirits as His eyes, Christ is searching all the churches and all the saints and also infusing Himself into the churches and the saints. On the one hand, we may fear His searching, but on the other hand, we should welcome it and be thankful for it because it is always followed by His infusing. Actually, His searching and His infusing go together, for His searching is accompanied by His infusing. As He searches us He infuses Himself into us.

We may experience this searching and infusing as we are praying. While we pray, the Lord searches us and infuses us with Himself. Suppose, for example, a brother speaks to his wife with right words but with a wrong spirit. Later, while he is praying, the Lord searches him and rebukes him for being wrong with his wife. The brother repents and says, "Lord, I was wrong with my wife, yet it is hard for me to repent to her and ask her to forgive me." However, the Lord not only searches and rebukes this brother but also infuses Himself into him. As a result of this infusing, the brother has the supply to go to his wife, confess, and ask for her forgiveness.

2. Saving the Believers

As the sevenfold intensified Spirit Christ saves the believers from the things related to the degradation of the church.

a. The Formal Church Life

The sevenfold intensified Spirit saves the believers from the formal church life, the loss of the first love to the Lord, the loss of the shining capacity of the lampstand, and the loss of the enjoyment of Christ as life in the church in Ephesus (2:1-7). The church in Ephesus had lost four things: the genuine and proper church life, the first love toward the

Lord, the shining capacity of the lampstand, and the enjoyment of Christ as life. Such a loss is very serious.

Some of the churches in the Lord's recovery may have lost these four things. Instead of a real and genuine church life, the saints in these churches have only a formal church life. The saints still love one another, but their love is quite formal. They do not have the real and genuine love toward the brothers. Furthermore, the saints in these churches still come to the meetings, but they attend the meetings merely in a formal way. A good number of saints have this kind of formality. We need to be genuine, and to be genuine is to be in the spirit and do everything in the spirit.

If we have lost our first love to the Lord, we will not be warm toward Him. Although we may continue to serve Him, we will be cold in our serving. We need to be saved from a formal church life and serve the Lord with a burning spirit (Rom. 12:11).

b. Defeat

The believers need to be saved by the seven Spirits from the defeat that leads to the taste of the second death spoken of in the Lord's word to the church in Smyrna (Rev. 2:8-11). Those who are defeated in the way described in verses 10 and 11 may taste of the second death, the lake of fire. We need to realize, therefore, that it is possible for a saved person to be hurt by the lake of fire as the second death.

c. Union with the World

The believers need to be saved also from the worldliness in union with the world as a marriage and the teaching of Balaam and the Nicolaitans in the church in Pergamos (vv. 12-17).

d. Fornication, Idolatry, and Demonic Teaching

Next, the sevenfold intensified Spirit saves the believers from the fornication, idolatry, demonic teaching, and satanic depths in Catholicism, signified by the church in Thyatira (vv. 18-29). In the Catholic Church today, there are many demonic teachings, for example, the teaching that one's prayers can shorten the time that someone else will spend in purgatory. Even though the Catholic Church correctly teaches certain things regarding God, Christ, and redemption, this teaching has been "leavened" by being mixed with pagan practices, heretical doctrines, and evil matters. Many of these are enumerated in the book entitled *The Two Babylons*.

e. Spiritual Death

Furthermore, the believers need to be saved from the spiritual death—from being dead and dying—in Protestantism, signified by the church in Sardis (3:1-6). Spiritual death is prevailing in today's Protestantism. Some in the denominations are quite good, but the majority are either dead or dying.

f. Losing the Crown

Next, the believers need to be saved from the losing of the crown, which has been gained already in Brethrenism, signified by the church in Philadelphia (vv. 7-13). *Philadelphia* means "brotherly love." Some in Brethrenism had gained the crown but eventually were defeated and were in danger of losing the crown at the Lord's coming back. Thus, the Lord warned them, saying, "Hold fast what you have that no one take your crown" (v. 11).

g. Lukewarmness and Christlessness

Finally, Christ as the sevenfold intensified Spirit saves the believers from the lukewarmness and the Christlessness in degraded Brethrenism, signified by the church in Laodicea (vv. 14-22). We know that the church in Laodicea was Christless by the fact that He was outside the church, standing at the door and knocking (v. 20). This indicates that we may have Christ in name but not in reality. We need to be careful lest this become our situation today. We all should consider these matters not for others but for ourselves.

3. The Means by Which the Believers Are Saved from Degradation

Now we need to see the means by which the believers are saved from the degradation of the church.

a. The Speaking of the Pneumatic Christ

Christ saves us from degradation by His speaking. In Revelation 2 and 3 the speaking of the unlimited life-releasing sevenfold intensified pneumatic Christ to the seven churches at the beginning of each epistle respectively becomes the speaking of the sevenfold intensified, all-inclusive, life-giving Spirit to all the seven churches at the end of each epistle universally (2:1, 7, 8, 11, 12, 17, 18, 29; 3:1, 6, 7, 13, 14, 22). At the beginning of each of the seven epistles, it is Christ who is speaking, but at the end of each epistle it is the Spirit who is speaking. The speaking of Christ therefore becomes the speaking of the Spirit. From this we see that Christ's speaking and the Spirit's speaking are one speaking. Christ speaks to a particular local church, and the Spirit speaks to the universal Body. By this speaking Christ saves us from the degradation of today's church.

b. The Participation of the Overcoming Saints

Christ saves the believers also by the participation of the overcoming saints who are living in their spirit drawn by the Lamb (1:10; 4:2; 17:3; 21:10; 14:4). Christ and the Spirit speak, and the overcoming saints respond and say yes to the Lord. The believers who respond in this way will be saved.

4. The Goal of the Intensified Work of God's Organic Salvation

For what are the believers saved from degradation by the sevenfold intensified Spirit? In order to answer this question, we need to see the goal of the intensified work of God's organic salvation.

a. Producing the Overcomers

This salvation is for producing the overcomers to build up the Body of Christ for the initial consummation of the New Jerusalem in the kingdom age (2:7) and the full consummation of the New Jerusalem in the new heaven and new earth (21:2). As we look at the situation of today's Christians, we may wonder who will build up the Body of Christ. Without the overcomers the Body of Christ cannot be built up, and unless the Body of Christ is built up, Christ cannot come back for His bride. Christ will come back not only as the Savior but also as the Bridegroom to marry His bride, who will be the totality of the overcomers. The building up of the Body of Christ is by the overcomers produced by God in the intensified work of His organic salvation.

The building up of the Body of Christ by the overcomers in this age is for the initial consummation of the New Jerusalem in the kingdom age and eventually for the full consummation of the New Jerusalem in the new heaven and new earth.

b. The Preparation of the Bride

The intensified work of God's organic salvation is also for the complete preparation of the bride of Christ so that the Bridegroom may have His triumphant wedding in the millennium for His satisfaction according to His good pleasure (19:7-9). John 3 indicates that Christ is the Bridegroom coming for the bride, who is composed of all the regenerated people. But nearly two thousand years have passed, and the bride still has not been prepared. The overcomers produced by Christ's intensified work will build up the Body of Christ, which will become the bride of Christ. Thus, Christ's wedding will take place as a result of His intensified work.

c. The Formation of the Bridal Army

Next, Christ's intensified work is for the formation of the bridal army for Christ to defeat and destroy His top enemies in humanity, the Antichrist and his false prophet (Rev. 19:11-21; 17:14). At the end of this age Antichrist and his false prophet will rise up to be the top enemies of Christ in humanity. Who will defeat them? These enemies will be defeated by Christ's bridal army, formed with the overcomers. Christ and His bride will fight against His human enemies and destroy them.

d. The Binding of Satan

Furthermore Christ's intensified work is for the binding of

Satan and the casting of him into the abyss for one thousand years (20:1-3).

e. The Bringing In of the Kingdom

Finally, Christ's intensified work is for the bringing in of the kingdom of Christ and of God which will be the millennium (vv. 4-6).

5. The Final Outcome

The final outcome of Christ's intensified work will be that the ultimately consummated Spirit as the consummation of the processed Triune God becomes the Bridegroom, and the aggregate of the overcoming saints becomes the bride of the universal romance between the redeeming God and His redeemed man as the conclusion of the entire Scriptures (22:17).

III. AN APPENDIX

The words, listed as follows, concerning the compounded, all-inclusive, life-giving, and indwelling Spirit, unveil also the secret of God's organic salvation:

A. The consummated Spirit as the second Paraclete (the Comforter), the realization of Christ as the first Paraclete, takes care of the believers, especially in the matter of the Divine Trinity being the main, life element of the organic salvation of God (John 14:16-18).

B. The indwelling Spirit joins in to help the believers in their weakness and He Himself intercedes by groaning in the spirit of the believers that all things may work together for good to those who love God that they may be conformed to the image of His Son that He might be the Firstborn among many brothers (Rom. 8:26, 28-29).

C. The believer who is joined to the Lord can experience the Lord to the climax, even to be one spirit with the Lord (God) (1 Cor. 6:17).

D. The Father strengthens the believers, according to the riches of His glory, with power through His Spirit into the believers' inner man, for Christ to make His home in the believers' heart that they may be filled unto the fullness of the Triune God for His corporate expression (Eph. 3:16-19). When Christ has the freedom to make His home in our heart, then we will be filled unto all the fullness of the Triune God to be the Body to express the Triune God corporately.

E. The apostle who sought to know Christ and gain Him was enabled to do all things in Christ who empowered him by His Spirit of bountiful supply (Phil. 3:10a, 12; 4:13; 1:19).

ABOUT THE AUTHOR

Witness Lee was born in 1905 in northern China and raised in a Christian family. At age 19 he was fully captured for Christ and immediately consecrated himself to preach the gospel for the rest of his life. Early in his service, he met Watchman Nee, a renowned preacher, teacher, and writer. Witness Lee labored together with Watchman Nee under his direction. In 1934 Watchman Nee entrusted Witness Lee with the responsibility for his publication operation, called the Shanghai Gospel Bookroom.

Prior to the Communist takeover in 1949, Witness Lee was sent by Watchman Nee and his other co-workers to Taiwan to ensure that the things delivered to them by the Lord would not be lost. Watchman Nee instructed Witness Lee to continue the former's publishing operation abroad as the Taiwan Gospel Bookroom, which has been publicly recognized as the publisher of Watchman Nee's works outside China. Witness Lee's work in Taiwan manifested the Lord's abundant blessing. From a mere 350 believers, newly fled from the mainland, the churches in Taiwan grew to 20,000 in five years.

In 1962 Witness Lee felt led of the Lord to come to the United States, and he began to minister in Los Angeles. During his 35 years of service in the U.S., he ministered in weekly meetings and weekend conferences, delivering several thousand spoken messages. Much of his speaking has since been published as over 400 titles. Many of these have been translated into over fourteen languages. He gave his last public conference in February 1997 at the age of 91.

He leaves behind a prolific presentation of the truth in the Bible. His major work, *Life-study of the Bible,* comprises over 25,000 pages of commentary on every book of the Bible from the perspective of the believers' enjoyment and experience of God's divine life in Christ through the Holy Spirit. Witness Lee was the chief editor of a new translation of the New Testament into Chinese called the Recovery Version and directed the translation of the same into English. The Recovery Version also appears in a number of other languages. He provided an extensive body of footnotes, outlines, and spiritual cross references. A radio broadcast of his messages can be heard on Christian radio stations in the United States. In 1965 Witness Lee founded Living Stream Ministry, a non-profit corporation, located in Anaheim, California, which officially presents his and Watchman Nee's ministry.

Witness Lee's ministry emphasizes the experience of Christ as life and the practical oneness of the believers as the Body of Christ. Stressing the importance of attending to both these matters, he led the churches under his care to grow in Christian life and function. He was unbending in his conviction that God's goal is not narrow sectarianism but the Body of Christ. In time, believers began to meet simply as the church in their localities in response to this conviction. In recent years a number of new churches have been raised up in Russia and in many European countries.

OTHER BOOKS PUBLISHED BY
Living Stream Ministry

Titles by Witness Lee:

Abraham—Called by God	978-0-7363-0359-0
The Experience of Life	978-0-87083-417-2
The Knowledge of Life	978-0-87083-419-6
The Tree of Life	978-0-87083-300-7
The Economy of God	978-0-87083-415-8
The Divine Economy	978-0-87083-268-0
God's New Testament Economy	978-0-87083-199-7
The World Situation and God's Move	978-0-87083-092-1
Christ vs. Religion	978-0-87083-010-5
The All-inclusive Christ	978-0-87083-020-4
Gospel Outlines	978-0-87083-039-6
Character	978-0-87083-322-9
The Secret of Experiencing Christ	978-0-87083-227-7
The Life and Way for the Practice of the Church Life	978-0-87083-785-2
The Basic Revelation in the Holy Scriptures	978-0-87083-105-8
The Crucial Revelation of Life in the Scriptures	978-0-87083-372-4
The Spirit with Our Spirit	978-0-87083-798-2
Christ as the Reality	978-0-87083-047-1
The Central Line of the Divine Revelation	978-0-87083-960-3
The Full Knowledge of the Word of God	978-0-87083-289-5
Watchman Nee—A Seer of the Divine Revelation ...	978-0-87083-625-1

Titles by Watchman Nee:

How to Study the Bible	978-0-7363-0407-8
God's Overcomers	978-0-7363-0433-7
The New Covenant	978-0-7363-0088-9
The Spiritual Man • 3 volumes	978-0-7363-0269-2
Authority and Submission	978-0-7363-0185-5
The Overcoming Life	978-1-57593-817-2
The Glorious Church	978-0-87083-745-6
The Prayer Ministry of the Church	978-0-87083-860-6
The Breaking of the Outer Man and the Release ...	978-1-57593-955-1
The Mystery of Christ	978-1-57593-954-4
The God of Abraham, Isaac, and Jacob	978-0-87083-932-0
The Song of Songs	978-0-87083-872-9
The Gospel of God • 2 volumes	978-1-57593-953-7
The Normal Christian Church Life	978-0-87083-027-3
The Character of the Lord's Worker	978-1-57593-322-1
The Normal Christian Faith	978-0-87083-748-7
Watchman Nee's Testimony	978-0-87083-051-8

Available at
Christian bookstores, or contact Living Stream Ministry
2431 W. La Palma Ave. • Anaheim, CA 92801
1-800-549-5164 • www.livingstream.com